ENOUGH FOR TODAY

Forty Reflections for Surviving the Wilderness

DONNA BARBER

ivp

An imprint of InterVarsity Press
Downers Grove, Illinois

InterVarsity Press
P.O. Box 1400 | Downers Grove, IL 60515-1426
ivpress.com | email@ivpress.com

InterVarsity Press® is the publishing division of InterVarsity Christian Fellowship/USA®. For more information, visit intervarsity.org.

All Scripture quotations, unless otherwise indicated, are taken from the AMPLIFIED Bible, copyright © 1954, 1958, 1962, 1965, 1987, 2015 by The Lockman Foundation. All rights reserved. Used by permission. www.lockman.org

While any stories in this book are true, some names and identifying information may have been changed to protect the privacy of individuals.

The publisher cannot verify the accuracy or functionality of website URLs used in this book beyond the date of publication.

Cover design: Faceout Studio, Molly von Borstel
Interior design: Jeanna Wiggins
Cover images: © altmodern / E+ via Getty Images, © CSA-Printstock / DigitalVision Vectors
          via Getty Images, © Zachary Domes / 500px Prime via Getty Images,
          © CSA-Images / Vetta via Getty Images

ISBN 978-1-5140-1254-3 (print) | ISBN 978-1-5140-1255-0 (digital)

Printed in the United States of America ⊖

Library of Congress Cataloging-in-Publication Data
A catalog record for this book is available from the Library of Congress.

31 30 29 28 27 26 25 | 13 12 11 10 9 8 7 6 5 4 3 2 1

"With the encouragement of a well-traveled guide, Donna Barber shares with vulnerability a way forward in the wilderness journeys of life. Her reflections, intertwined with personal experience and the truths of the Christian faith, clearly demonstrate her own lived resilience, patience, and hope. Wilderness experiences are inevitable. Barber's words assure you that finding yourself in the wilderness is not a result of steps on a mistaken path but are instead important and defining moments of a life lived with purpose."

Michelle Ferrigno Warren, activist and author of *Join the Resistance* and *The Power of Proximity*

"In *Enough for Today*, Donna Barber expands our view of manna beyond physical nourishment to reveal the multifaceted ways God's provision unfolds. Through personal narrative, she serves as a beacon for those seeking sustenance in these challenging times. Grounded in Scripture, *Enough for Today* reminds us that God meets us in the full depth and breadth of our humanity as image bearers. Reading this text encouraged my faith, and I'm confident that readers will become more trusting and attuned to the abundant ways God provides."

José Humphreys III, author of *Seeing Jesus in East Harlem* and *Ecosystems of Jubilee*

"Donna Barber has done it again! In *Enough for Today*, she gives us all the encouragement we need to keep going during trying times. This is a biblically based, contextually relevant, and extremely timely group of devotionals which weary sojourners can return to many times."

Jonathan "Pastah J" Brooks, lead pastor of Lawndale Christian Community Church and author of Church Forsaken

———————————

To my faithful sister-friends,

Jamie Noling-Auth, Velynn Brown, Raina Evans, and Andrea Scott,

whose persistent encouragement and accountability

willed this book into being.

———————————

To my Portland Groves Church family

for making space for me and my gifts, physical and emotional,

during this writing project.

———————————

To my husband and partner, Leroy Barber,

who walks beside me through the wilderness and the mountaintops

of this life, holding my hand and cheering me on. I love you.

———————————

CONTENTS

Introduction: Living on Manna 1

PART ONE: DISCOVERING GOD

1. As Abba Father 9

2. As Close as Song 12

3. Dios Habla en Español 15

4. God as Fire 19

5. God as Sunshine 23

6. God as Spirit 27

7. God as Word 31

8. As Sweet Water 34

9. In Grief and Joy 38

10. In the Silence 42

PART TWO: DISCOVERING CALL

11. God Calling 49

12. Imposter Syndrome 52

13. I Am the Way 55

14. Submersion Is Submission 58

15. Hungry in the Far Country 62

16. Take Courage 66

17. In Faith or Obedience 69

18. Peace Out 73

19. "Do You Love Me?" 77

20. For the Prize 80

PART THREE: FACING FEAR

21. Lord of the Darkness 85

22. Flats Happen 89

23. Pressing On 92

24. Sometimes the Wilderness Calls for an Unfair Fight 96

25. Trusting God Is a Decision 99

26. By Hell or Whitewater 102

27. Found in the Wild 106

28. This Midnight 109

29. The Wilderness Is Not Safe 112

30. By Another Name 116

PART FOUR: FINDING OURSELVES

31. Costumes and Cosplay 121

32. Learning to Sing in a Strange Land 125

33. A Familiar Feast 128

34. Sabbath 132

35. And One for All 135

36. From Faith to Faith 138

37. Hero Capes and Camouflage 141

38. Finding Faith in a Foreign Land 144

39. Let There Be Rain 148

40. Mirrors 152

Epilogue: Crossing Jordan 155

Notes 158

Introduction

LIVING ON MANNA

JESUS SAID TO THE BAPTIST, do this thing that I'm telling you to do. It may not make sense. It doesn't seem right or fitting, but do it anyway. In doing so you will fulfill all of what is right. And the heavens opened and the Father spoke and the Spirit descended. Hallelujah!

The next thing we know, Jesus is led by the Spirit into the wilderness to be tempted by the devil. The road to freedom and new life is often through the wilderness. The road through the wilderness begins with the waters of baptism and death. Dying to what was and can never, should never, be again. Dying to the slave that we were.

For many of us the past years have felt heavy with the plagues of illness and dying, anger and violence, fires and wrath. And numerous pharaohs, from the church house to the courthouse to the White House, have risen up to withstand the move of God toward freedom and new life for his people. But YHWH will not be denied.

We often talk about "clinging desperately to life" and "letting go" in death. The road through the wilderness begins with baptism, dying, letting go of the trauma and hurt of the past. As we are plunged down into the waters of our own death, we must let go of the slave that we were—of slave thinking and doing and ways of being. We close our eyes, take a deep breath, and release ourselves into the strong, capable hands and arms of the Baptizer.

In one full swoosh the water covers us, like the dirt of the grave. A moment later we come up dripping with the waters of new life. Our eyes open, we find our feet beneath us, and we take in that first breath. Now strong hands reach down to pull us upward and out, and the water that rolls down our cheeks mixes with the salty tears of joy. Then often, like Jesus, we step out of the pool or onto the banks of the river and into the wilderness.

More than twenty-five years ago, I drove out of the city of my birth and rebirth, Philadelphia, and into the wilderness of Atlanta, Georgia. I didn't know where I was headed. I didn't realize what lay ahead. Still, the road to my freedom began on the I-95 south interstate highway.

For a follower of Jesus, the wilderness is a place of testing, a special place where our identity as the people of God is established. It is the period when we are questioned by the enemy and the world and even ourselves on who we are and what we believe. It is a place of trial and temptation, discomfort and thirst. It is a place between. Between death and resurrection, between the inhale and the exhale. Between Egypt and the Promised Land.

The wilderness can also be a time apart when we are separated from comfort and familiarity. The people and landmarks we know have fallen away and the way ahead is unclear. When we packed our children and all we could carry into the back of a minivan and headed south, we were giddy and excited to begin the new adventure. But when we arrived in our new city, eight hundred miles from our old life, there was no party or friends to receive us. Our new "home" was littered with trash and boards covered the windows. Our van was soon stolen and the people we came to join were all away on vacation. We spent our first nights angry and disoriented, sleeping on bunks in the basement of an empty building belonging to the new "ministry" we came to serve. Wilderness.

The protests and marches over the years have led many through the path of a vast sea that cannot be recrossed. We have left the work and ways of a colonized life and faith on the other side, but the fertile land of promise appears still a long way off in the not yet. So, we are left in this present wilderness of now. Mud on our feet, dust in our mouths, arms tired and backs sore.

> The whole congregation of the Israelites [grew discontented and] murmured and rebelled against Moses and Aaron in the wilderness, and the Israelites said to them, "Would that we had died by the hand of the LORD in the land of Egypt, when we sat by the pots of meat and ate bread until we were full; for you have brought us out into this wilderness to kill this entire assembly with hunger."
>
> Then the LORD said to Moses, "Behold, I will cause bread to rain from heaven for you; the people shall go out and gather a day's portion every day, so that I may test them [to determine] whether or not they will walk [obediently] in My instruction (law)." (Exodus 16:2-4)

Two and a half months after leaving Egypt, the Israelites entered the wilderness. With their food and energy depleted, they began to grumble and complain. The suffering and oppression of Egypt had faded in their minds, and many began to long for the good old days of slavery where at least they could count on the overseer's food. Instead, God himself provided food for his people, raining down manna, bread from heaven, each morning. Just enough to nourish them for the day. Through this small prescribed act of obedience, the Lord began to shift their thinking and their dependence from humanity to the living God. They had to lie down each night storing nothing for the future other than a growing faith in the one who promised to provide.

There is no map for the wilderness, no street signs or rest stops with snacks. No Siri with a clear indication of how long it will be or how far you have yet to go. But in the wilderness, stripped of our distractions, we remember or discover our God. Divorced from the empire's daily rations, we must look to God to be bread. We can welcome that dryness that we feel in our throats knowing that Jesus said within us we carry a well of water springing up into everlasting life.

I do not know the boundaries of your wilderness, when it began or how long it will last. But this book is meant to be a tool for your journey—a daily devotional pause for reflection to remind you of what is true and honest, just, pure, and lovely, and despite this present darkness, still worthy of praise. Many of us are familiar with the imagery of the wilderness as a place of testing. But it can also be, as we prayerfully traverse each section of this book, an invitation to discover God and calling, face our fears, and more deeply understand ourselves. It is an encouragement to look for a God who shows up in the pillars of cloud and fire and the burning bushes of our everyday lives to speak to, guide, and protect us. In this space between what was and what shall be, we must pause each day to read, pray, and drink from the well. For it is the sword of the Spirit, the

Word of the living God, that will prepare us for and take us through the days of testing ahead.

When the journey becomes too much, perhaps we find ourselves in the wilderness like the prophet Elijah. Thankfully, our God provides manna for days like these, and it will be enough.

Then the angel of the LORD came again a second time and touched him and said, "Get up, and eat, for the journey is too long for you [without adequate sustenance]. So he got up and ate and drank, and with the strength of that food he traveled forty days and nights to Horeb (Sinai), the mountain of God. (1 Kings 19:7-8)

Arise and eat.

Part One

DISCOVERING GOD

1

AS ABBA FATHER

The Spirit Himself testifies and confirms together with our
spirit [assuring us] that we [believers] are children of God.

ROMANS 8:16

SUPPOSE I WAS FORTUNATE to grow up, for the most part, in a two-parent home. My parents met, married, and then separated and reconciled many times over the course of my childhood. My dad was complicated. A black man, born in the twenties and raised in the South with an eighth-grade education. He entered the army in 1943 during World War II. Then, after receiving an honorable discharge, he returned to eventually meet and marry my mother and settle down in the northern city of Philadelphia. He ended up finding work as a weaver in a local textile mill. He worked hard five days a week and partied in the local speakeasy throughout the weekend.

He was not warm or affectionate toward me. But I suspect now, through my grown-up understanding, that perhaps his life did not allow him to be. Still, I think I desired some form of meaningful connection with him. Instead I settled for the occasional walk with him to the neighborhood deli to pick up a "cold one," my short legs scrambling to match his long stride.

Other than this and the financial rewards I received for my straight-A report cards, I felt largely unseen by him. He reserved most of his energy for his gruff interactions with my mother. She complained about money and he complained about her lack of cooking and unwavering devotion to the church. He was not what my child's mind expected a father to be—protector, provider, loving comfort, or playful friend. I needed him to shape and affirm my beauty and character. To make me feel safe and loved. To tell me everything would be all right and to make it so. Unfortunately, broken, flawed, and limited by what appeared to me a godless life, he could not be what I needed him to be.

Thankfully, I met God as Father, the big, strong presence speaking to me through Word and Spirit of unconditional love. I met God as Father with promises of protection and provision that only he could fulfill. I met God as Father, a daily comfort and abiding peace for my worst days and my best days and all the excruciatingly hard and beautiful hours and moments in between. I met God as Father and found him to be the perfect, immutable parent I needed him to be.

Now, of course, I understand God in these more recent years in other forms and expressions. For God too is like a mother, the giver of new life and the Creator of all things. I am acquainted with the triune God, uniquely three in the divine One. And I recognize that God as Spirit is not housed in, confined to, or limited by human gender, masculine, feminine, or any other. I know that God was not conceived or born like a man in time and therefore has no beginning and no end but is, was, and is yet to be. The Almighty.

I also acknowledge that for some, the image of God as Father feels foreign. It may conjure decidedly negative associations that tempt you to resist God or walk away. The gift of grace, however, is that while God may be consistent across a broad range of experiences and understandings (Creator, love, truth, etc.), God is also uniquely distinct to us as individuals in the express ways we need God to be. Which allows us to discover ourselves, remember ourselves, to be precisely who we were meant to be and to reflect that understanding to the people we encounter in our lives.

God revealed himself to that little West Philly girl as Abba Father, not because he was limited to that expression by any patriarchal colonial representation. I met God as Father for the same reason God showed up as a burning bush for Moses, an angelic army surrounding Elisha, and a bright light for pre-converted Paul. Because in the chaos of our daily lives, God in love appears expressly as we need him to be.

2

AS CLOSE AS SONG

I MET GOD FIRST AS MUSIC. Song lyrics and Bible text were often one and the same for me. When I was three years old, my mother took me to my first children's choir rehearsal because she said I was always singing. I was too young to read or properly dress myself, but I quickly learned the lyrics and melody of any song I heard. Fortunately, our church children's choir had a repertoire of music that was rich with Scripture, so before I could read the Bible, I was singing it.

By the age of six I got my first solo in our annual Good Friday cantata. Not long after that, it was the lead in a musical version of the beatitudes. This song, along with many others, laid a scriptural foundation in my heart. I hummed and sang and tapped their rhythm again and again, on my way to school, before I went to bed, even lying on the exam table at the doctor's office. I sang when I was happy and when I was sad. And thanks to the breadth of musical genres in my black Baptist church, I learned to sing and appreciate a variety of musical styles and cultural expressions. Through standard hymns and gospel rhythms as well as the four-part harmonies of Negro spirituals and classical anthems, I learned not only what God said but who God was and who I was because of him.

From processional to recessional, music helped me experience God. He was big and powerful like the thundering strains of the pipe organ and gentle and comforting like a chanted prayer. The thump and cadence of five hundred feet against the wood floor resonated throughout the sanctuary, bringing us into step with a holy God and one another, taking us back to something ancient. Bare feet on hushed harbor soil and holy ground.

In my childhood church, God spoke to us in the tearful shrill of the soprano solo and in the pounding chords, rounded harmonies, and clapping hands of a well-robed choir. The music was the backdrop and driver of every occasion. The connector of head, heart, and body with soul and Spirit, deepening every message.

When Israel watched the armies of Egypt covered by the waters of the Red Sea, Moses and the people of Israel broke out into singing. It is the first recorded song in the Bible (Exodus 15). The Hebrew women took up timbrels and began dancing, and Miriam, the prophetess, sang a song of triumph. Likewise, in the music of my black church, I came to know God in the joy of celebration. Hands raised, feet dancing, bodies moving in worship and praise. We celebrated weddings and anniversaries, homecomings, homegoings, prayers answered, and lives reborn. But mostly we celebrated our survival. Another year, another week, another day. Despite the army of troubles assembled against us, we remained, and God met us as celebration in the call and response of our songs.

God also met us in the music of our pain, through the black keys of the piano and the blue notes of the refrain. I met God in the music of lament and through the darker tones of grief. When the world was hard and cold or difficult to understand, God was present in the dissonance of my frustrations and the brooding songs of my heart. Jesus, the man of sorrows, was acquainted with my grief and made this known to me through the words and the notes and the rhythm of the music.

God showed up outside the church walls in the smoke of jazz and blues, in the soulful voices of R&B, through the electronics of funk, the storytelling of rap, and the global wildfire that is hip-hop. Through every genre, in every key, God is in the music, speaking through and past the lyrics to the joy and pain of my life and the rhythm of my heartbeat.

Just after the Red Sea celebrations, Moses and the children of Israel entered the wilderness of Shur and spent three days in the desert without water. Music prepares the mind and body for the challenges of suffering. It quiets our nervous system, reduces stress hormones, increases blood flow, and lowers blood pressure. Jehovah-Rapha, the God who heals, meets us in the wonder and power of music and comforts us with his song.

Miriam danced. David played. Mary sang. In the end, the saints of God will rejoice. Despite whatever has happened or ever will, God shows up in the music of our time as strength and joy and hope. We may need to close our eyes and hum the tune a bit to remember the words, but before too long, we will find the beat (and perhaps ourselves) and again sing along.

3

DIOS HABLA EN ESPAÑOL

There is one body [of believers] and one Spirit—just as you were
called to one hope when called [to salvation]—one Lord, one
faith, one baptism, one God and Father of us all who is [sovereign]
over all and [working] through all and [living] in all.

EPHESIANS 4:4-6

I N THE SMALL, LARGELY HOMOGENOUS bubbles of our families, churches, or communities, it is easy to imagine that God is one of us, made in our image with similar likes, dislikes, and pleasures. That she listens to hip-hop or R&B old school, watches cheesy rom-com movies or reality TV, prefers sweet potato pie and collards over pumpkin and green bean casserole. I met God in the foot-stomping, hand-clapping, sing-and-sway of the black church with occasional visits to the televised words of Dr. Charles Stanley. But in the fall of 1995, we ventured across the border and the walls of our understanding to visit new friends then living and serving in Mexico City.

We did a few typical tourist things like visiting a festival and the pyramids at Teotihuacán. But mostly we spent time immersed in the daily lives of our friends—a doctor and economists—as they brought medical care and economic development to the struggling communities near their home.

I don't remember quite what I expected before boarding the plane. Only that it was exciting and terrifying all at once. But once there, I was struck by the size and the enormous population of the city and the profound panorama of poverty. Seeing and visiting places without electricity or running water and the many large families living in tiny tin handmade homes. But again and again I was equally struck by something else—the beauty and rich culture of the Mexican people. Despite the challenges of their living conditions, they embodied a pride, generosity, and hospitality that we felt wherever we went. From the creative young entrepreneurs who hopped on and off the many forms of mass transit selling their wares to the husband and father who insisted on spending the equivalent of a week's wages to buy cold sodas for our family of five. Time and again, we who were foreigners and strangers, different in looks and language and culture, were greeted with warmth and kindness and treated as honored guests.

Throughout our stay we saw few if any people who looked like us. Yet our differentness was greeted with smiles and friendly gestures in the absence of common words. Our three brown children became quick celebrities in each marketplace we visited, and they responded with waves and smiles in kind. Miles away from the negative racial stigmas of the States, we bathed in an unfamiliar appreciation of our own unique beauty. Our textured hair, curvy bodies, and brown skin were viewed with interest and admiration rather than offense or rejection, and we welcomed the change.

On a wealthier side of town, I got to attend a small women's Bible study. Then later we joined in an evening worship service at our friends' church. At the beginning of the service my friend whispered a steady interpretation of the various speakers to aid my understanding of all that was happening and being said. However, before too long, he was caught up in the power of the message and fell off with interpreting, and I was left to listen at first without ears to hear. But soon the spoken word gave way to singing, and the music began to move my body and stir my soul. All around me people sang or whispered prayers in worship and, though the language was unfamiliar, the Spirit was well known.

Santo, santo, santo
Santo, santo, santo
Santo, santo, santo
Yo quiero verte.

I met God on the pew of a church in Mexico City, through the words of a language I didn't understand, and he was bigger than I had ever seen or experienced before. Yet this God was not new but rather a fuller expression of the same being I had always known, just more fully revealed. In Mexico I discovered God's transcendence across all our human barriers of maps and borders, political parties and denominations. He is imprinted on the faces and shows up in the cultural expressions of every people and land that has been named.

God is not confined to any individual church or seminary classroom, and the knowledge of him is not limited to those with the privilege to find belonging or access in such places. God is found and known by those who seek him. God is revealed to the Jew and the Gentile, the slave and the free, through old women and young children, within the ivy-covered gates of the lecture hall and the graffiti-tagged walls of the 'hood.

I met God in the southern barrios of North America standing on dirt floors under tin roofs. Through the generosity of strangers, the sweetness of hot, chocolate-filled churros, and the prayers of the righteous spoken, sung, and whispered in love to a God who speaks Spanish.

4

GOD AS FIRE

N THE THROES OF MARRIAGE and young motherhood, I met the Lord as fire. Not in the romantic glow of hearth and candlelight or the comforting flames of the kind of campfire that warms our faces and roasts our marshmallows. No, I came to know God the way the writer of Hebrews declares him to be—as consuming fire, cleansing, purging, refining.

After we say yes to call, the work begins. We set out on a path toward new life but are often weighted down with all that we were, all that we had, all that we knew. We step toward new life carrying the carcass of our former self and quickly become exhausted under the strain. Despite our excited talk about freedom, we cannot imagine its breadth. So we cling to old plans and old boundaries. We attempt to build new temples with outdated tools. We try to cast new vision with outmoded descriptors and quickly find ourselves stalled in frustration.

> "Come to Me, all who are weary and heavily burdened [by religious rituals that provide no peace], and I will give you rest [refreshing your souls with salvation]." (Matthew 11:28)

The initial call came in the late eighties. As a new wife and then a young mother, I was just settling into family life as we imagined it. We had found a cute little apartment, birthed a bubbly baby girl, landed decent jobs, and had respectable roles in comfortable church-based ministry. But God drew our attention and then our hearts to the suffering of those living in the discomfort of homelessness, to relatives struggling with the discomfort of poverty, and communities of children trapped in systemic miseducation. As we said yes to serving and yes to giving and yes to addressing injustice, God began to strip away the trappings of our old lives piece by piece.

We lost the cute apartment in the perfect neighborhood when we took in a family member's children. I gave up my job to stay at home to care for them and my own. A few years later, my husband felt called to leave his full-time job to give more time to our nonprofit ministry to houseless neighbors. And shortly after, we learned we were expecting child number three. We were pressing toward tomorrow while being dragged under the weights of yesterday.

> Now this [expression], "Yet once more," indicates the removal and final transformation of all those things which can be shaken . . . so that those things which cannot be shaken may remain. Therefore, since we receive a kingdom which cannot be shaken, let us show gratitude, and offer to God pleasing service and acceptable worship with reverence and awe; for our God is [indeed] a consuming fire. (Hebrews 12:27-29)

I met God as fire, spreading swiftly through the brush of my life, clearing, purging, and burning off the dross of my mind. Cutting away the have-to's, must-do's, and shoulds of my thinking and the actual constraints that kept me tied to the small and the practical and the seemingly necessary.

"Your house is on fire!"

I stared in confusion at the familiar face outside the window of my small office. He was yelling, but it took a moment for the words to register. Ben, the facilities manager at the small nonprofit school where I worked, was yelling words I knew but found difficult to comprehend.

"Your house is on fire!" he yelled again, and this time the words landed with impact. I thought of my husband and two-year-old son whom I'd left at home earlier that morning and began heading for the door.

By the time I traveled the one-block distance to my home, the flames were just about out. What had not been consumed by fire had been taken by water or smoke. A neighbor held my son, and my husband sat nearby in tears. I listened to the many compassionate words of friends and neighbors through a fog, nodding and expressing thanks appropriately but largely disconnected. I was aware that I should be devastated. I understood that, as renters without insurance, all we owned had been lost. Still, as we gathered our older children from school and climbed into the back of a friend's car to accept their invitation of temporary housing, I felt something else I was too embarrassed at the time to admit. I felt free.

Just a few years later we would leave that house, that city, that life for good to begin again somewhere new.

Throughout Scripture, God is revealed as fire—a pillar by night, a burning bush on a mountain, tongues of fire at Pentecost. If we yield to the fire, he consumes the old things and the dead things and the things that drag us down yet we find difficult to release. I met God as fire, consuming all that entangled and held me bound. Burning off that which was unlike him. Igniting all I was yet to be. In the heat of that blaze, like the Hebrew boys in the fiery furnace, we discover something more lovely and more valuable than anything lost. Immanuel. The very presence of God.

5

GOD AS SUNSHINE

For the LORD God is a sun and shield;
The LORD bestows grace and favor and honor;
No good thing will He withhold from
those who walk uprightly.

PSALM 84:11

I MET GOD ONCE AS SUNSHINE. A warm, bright, closer-than-it-appears presence, beaming down at me from just above the row houses that formed my city block. The neighborhood market was just two blocks away, a short walk from my front door. But when I was a child, any venture alone off the block seemed scary and fraught with potential danger. Still, it was common to hear the voices of our mothers calling us in from play to go to the local market to get a loaf of bread or a gallon of milk, a lightbulb, a roll of toilet paper, or some other similar item that was discovered to be of necessity in the moment.

In the rules of community life in the city, that meant grabbing one or two or four of your good friends to walk with you, because in that group we were strong and safe and, most importantly, not alone. So in Philly it was common to see a whole group of chatty girls bopping to the corner store or neighborhood market to get a single loaf of bread. Because the task was easier, the walk shorter, the way less threatening in the community of friends.

But every now and then a mom would call for a store run when the block was empty. And since it was long before texting was even a thing of imagination, we actually walked, in person, up to the doors of our friends with the familiar request, "Can you walk me to the store?" If it was at all possible, your friend would agree, grateful for the company or the opportunity to get out of the house or conscious of the many times they'd had to make a similar request.

Still there were occasional times when it was necessary to make the walk alone. When no response came to a knock on the door or everyone was busy with chores or watching siblings or "on punishment" due to some infraction previously committed. At those times the short two blocks felt like a long two miles and the normally joyful chatter was replaced with a lonely, nervous silence.

This was before AirPods were available to fill the silence with sound, creating the familiar bubbles of personal space we all now know and enjoy. Before the time when computers fit into our pockets and entertainment was something summoned from a cloud. No, a walk through the city meant engaging with the neighborhood. Feeling feet on concrete, greeting neighbors, and even nodding to passing strangers.

For an introverted kid who hadn't yet found her voice, I found myself dreading these walks. I was afraid of running into the school bully alone or the menacing kids from the next block or the roving

eyes of teenage boys and old men on a body that seemed to be de-
veloping way too soon. I felt exposed and small and unprotected.

Until the day God showed up for me as sunshine, a warm and
comforting presence just above me. I squinted at that bright orb in
the sky and for the first time felt it as more. It was a smile and a hug,
rays of comfort and assurance that I was not, was never, alone. It was
a beam of protection above me and beside me. It was Father and
shelter and much-needed friend. I felt the smile of God on my face
in the sunshine, like a warm kiss on my cheek and an arm around
my shoulders. I heard the whisper of his promise move through my
ear and into my spirit, saying, "Even to the end of the age." I smiled
back and walked just a little bit taller, my steps no longer timid but
sure. I moved in the confidence of a faith found most often in
children, accepting without question what I knew with certainty to
be true.

For an adult, faith is often dimmed with reason and doubt and
fear. The evil of the world overshadows what we know to be the
truth of God. We abandon a faith that conflicts with human phi-
losophy or are misled by faulty teaching and the deceitfulness of
men. Some have chosen the path of painful experience over the
wisdom of instruction. Others, beaten down by disappointment and
circumstance, have lost hope and drifted or walked away. But the
God we knew as children is still real, and childlike faith is yet
faith indeed.

The God who made the earth and heavens showed up that day as
sunshine on my walk to the market, a bright, hot light in the sky, just
above the roofline of the row houses on my block. Just as real as the
body and blood of Communion. Just as close as Mary's breath on her

infant's face. Just as sure as John's declaration, "Behold the Lamb of God," and just as true as the Word made flesh he has always been.

O LORD of hosts,
How blessed and greatly favored is the man who trusts in You
[believing in You, relying on You, and committing himself to
You with confident hope and expectation]. (Psalm 84:12)

5

GOD AS SPIRIT

But a time is coming and is already here

when the true worshipers will worship the Father

in spirit [from the heart, the inner self] and in truth.

JOHN 4:23

MET GOD AS A STILL, small voice, separate from my own, yet speaking distinctly inside me. Gentle and reassuring, firm and corrective, warm and inviting, soft and consoling.

In the beginning, before God said, "Let there be . . . ," the Spirit of God moved over the face of the waters. Jesus was led, writes John, by the Spirit into the wilderness after his baptism. Simeon was prompted by the Spirit to enter the temple to meet the Christ child. It was the Spirit who led Philip to join the chariot of the Ethiopian official to share the gospel, and it was the Spirit who led Elizabeth to exclaim to Mary, "Blessed are you among women and blessed is the fruit of your womb!"

Throughout Scripture and history, the Spirit of the living God has been active, breathing and moving upon creation and humankind to accomplish the will of Almighty God in the earth. And since the day of Pentecost, the Holy Spirit has fallen on, come beside, and made home within the believer to lead and guide us to divine truth.

I met God as unction, a divine influence, pulling me, urging me forward. A thought that materializes with drive and urgency, to speak or do or move in a particular way and time. He is the inspiration and breath behind every good word, the instruction for every perfect act or deed.

In the reason and practicality of our modern understanding, some of us have put God on mute to be heard only through the latest popular bestseller or the twenty-minute window of the Sunday morning sermon. But God is always speaking, and as Lord of all things has all creation at his disposal. God speaks through his Word and his people but also echoes and flows through music, media, nature, astronomy, and even math. God, at work in our everyday lives, still shows up as the mystery and wonder of the Holy Ghost but is often dismissed as "feeling," "intuition," "red flag," or "passing thought." We sometimes ignore the leading and guidance of the Spirit of Truth, opting rather for popular opinion and the natural wisdom of the day.

Hollywood likes to portray the move of the Spirit in the black church as random, manic movement or the tool of charismatic leaders for fraudulent manipulation leaving many believers ashamed or embarrassed. But some of us have met and experienced the Holy Spirit as power, moving in us and through us, connecting us to God and one another.

In times of desperation and fear, when we have exhausted our natural resources and come to the end of ourselves, it is often then that we turn to the foolishness of preaching. As we hear the groans of creation through climate change, we bow our heads. As we watch the reports of war and see "evil men and impostors . . . go on from bad to worse" (2 Timothy 3:13), we close our eyes and call out to the unseen God for help. As the economy breaks down and our bodies wear out, we ask for instructions and search the silence for a sign.

I remember lying on the table of the cold procedure room as my doctor performed a breast biopsy, awake because I was six months pregnant with my second child and general anesthesia posed too great a threat to our unborn son. The night before I had lain awake listening to the voice of the enemy trying to convince me that I would die before I ever saw my child. In the light of day I was at peace, calmed by the Spirit of God that filled the room and whispered blessed assurance in my left ear until the procedure was done and a benign result received not long after.

Some of us, having packed up our toys and stomped away from God and church as we knew it, now stand searching the darkness of the void. Here, in the terror and grief of it all, we remember. We remember how we met God, who he was before. We remember how we met God as unfathomable joy or profound peace or the knot at the end of our fraying rope. We remember who we were before we became all-knowing. We breathe into the memory of his presence and long for the familiar comfort and reassurance of that still, small voice. Thankfully, no matter how far away we have traveled, when we turn our hearts back toward him, God is right there.

> God is spirit [the Source of life, yet invisible to mankind], and those who worship Him must worship in spirit and truth. (John 4:24)

I met and know God as Spirit, the resurrection power freeing me from the pain and disappointments of the past and as the abiding fellowship guiding me through the challenges that still lie ahead.

For all who are allowing themselves to be led by the Spirit of God are sons of God. (Romans 8:14)

¶

GOD AS WORD

IN MY EARLY TEENS I met God as the Word. He came to me in the familiar surroundings of the church sanctuary, spilling from the mouth of the preacher in the morning service. Before then, I had not seen or heard him as proclamation. Only through the lyric and melody of song.

I do not remember the details of that sermon, only that it captured my attention, drawing in my wandering young mind from browsing through the Baptist hymnals, counting light fixtures, or doodling on the back of the morning program. For the first time I zeroed in on a story formerly unknown to me and an application not yet considered. Something was quickened in me and I wanted to know more.

Not long after that experience, I began attending a youth Bible study made mandatory by the leaders of the popular youth choir I had joined. The church leaders had assigned a young, passionate minister to teach the class. I approached it with little expectation as my previous experiences with church Sunday school classes had been disappointing. I had lost interest in the rehearsal of the same, familiar children's Bible stories—Noah and the ark, Jonah and the whale, the Genesis story of creation—and so had abandoned the Sunday classes years before.

However, my initial reluctance quickly dissolved as I was drawn in by the young preacher. Rather than stories of one-time miraculous events that had occurred thousands of years before, he spoke of a God who was alive and active in the lives of his people today. More than that, he spoke like he knew this God and was known by him. He talked about who he was, not just what he did. More than the meek and mild shepherd, he talked about a Lion, a powerful God who cared for me, was pursuing me, and wanted to use me in his divine plan for the world.

I became intrigued and excited by this new information, this expanded representation of the God I thought I knew. I attended these Bible studies faithfully and then greedily devoured the Book throughout the week that followed. The Bible was not just an old book but a living text that spoke to my hungry heart about a God I now realized I barely knew. More than that, I was finding myself in its pages. While Jesus was revealing himself as door and bread and light and life, I was discovering Donna as light and salt and child and friend of God. I was a poor brown girl living in an urban center in the post-civil rights era of America in the 1970s. Black was beautiful, and Jesse Jackson and the Rainbow Coalition were shouting, "I am somebody" through my television screen. But here was the God of the universe adding an exclamation point, declaring through his Word and foreknowledge that I was loved, I was chosen, I was his. That I had a power given not by the laws of state but by the mouth of God through the blood of the Lamb, a resurrection power that could not be taken away.

God is not contained by the Book but rather revealed through it. John said,

In the beginning [before all time] was the Word (Christ), and the Word was with God, and the Word was God Himself. He was [continually existing] in the beginning [co-eternally] with God. All things were made and came into existence through Him; and without Him not even one thing was made that has come into being. . . .

But to as many as did receive and welcome Him, He gave the right [the authority, the privilege] to become children of God, *that is*, to those who believe in (adhere to, trust in, and rely on) His name—who were born, not of blood [natural conception], nor of the will of the flesh [physical impulse], nor of the will of man [that of a natural father], but of God [that is, a divine and supernatural birth—they are born of God— spiritually transformed, renewed, sanctified]. (John 1:1-3, 12-13)

The more I learned, the more I wanted to know this God, this Savior, this King. Through each sermon preached, each Scripture sung, every chapter, verse, and word read, I was being made whole, made new, made over. My mind was coming alive. My imagination and hope enlarged.

Your words were found and I ate them,
And your words became a joy to me and the delight of
    my heart;
For I have been called by Your name,
O Lord God of hosts. (Jeremiah 15:16)

I met God as the Word—a powerful, creative, revealing force that challenged and troubled and healed me. That made me new. And nothing would ever be the same.

8

AS SWEET WATER

T MUST HAVE BEEN QUITE SOMETHING, the sight of all those Egyptian chariots pouring off the shore down onto the floor of the Red Sea like so many rows of ants. The vision of all those soldiers, faces contorted in anger, bodies straining forward in vengeful determination. The sound of all those horses, hooves pounding, manes flying as they raced toward the Israelites under the insistence of the whips. It must have been a sight to behold—right up until the hand of God released the fury of the waves to cover them like the loose dirt of a grave.

Then the music started. The timbrels played. The people danced and the women sang songs of joy and freedom.

> Sing to the LORD, for He has triumphed gloriously and is highly exalted;
> The horse and its rider He has hurled into the sea. (Exodus 15:21)

And Israel marched forward into next, into the wilderness of Shur where, after three days of finding no drinkable water, their songs of freedom and triumph turned to murmuring and complaint.

The wilderness is a place of testing, a proving ground for what we think we know. Just a short time in its heat, cold, and darkness, many forget the power and goodness of God. The wilderness is a time of transition and transformation, of dying and rebirth. It is a season of forgetting and learning, a journey from bound to free, and can last from forty days to forty years.

For four hundred years Israel groaned under the oppression of Egypt, but while they lived under the distorted tyranny of slavery, rations became reasonable, and for some, slave masters became familiar frenemies. For Israel, the desert was a place of unlearning and of discovering a God they thought they already knew.

I often wondered why, when Pharoah wavered, God "hardened Pharoah's heart." Now, after struggling through my own battles of faith, I consider that while after six plagues Pharoah may have been ready to relent, God knew that Israel was not ready to be free. Perhaps plagues seven through ten were as much for them as for the stubborn Egyptian leader. They needed to know that God was bigger and more powerful than Pharoah and capable of protecting them from his wrath. So perhaps the first test was walking out of Egypt, which was made easier after the death of the Egyptian firstborn.

However, while they trusted God to protect them, could they rely on him to provide in the dry, barren land of the wilderness? While held in captivity, they were nourished by the fertile land of Egypt and the provision of their taskmasters. In the heat of the desert, confronted with thirst and the bitter undrinkable waters of Marah, they looked to another man, Moses, and questioned him regarding their thirst.

How many of us are murmuring in the newfound freedom of our day? We have left the lush lands of our former church plantations in hopes of a more just Promised Land. Yet we find ourselves traipsing through the dust of a spiritual wilderness in need of water and in search of bread. But God is interested in freeing more than our bodies. Mind and spirit must also be redeemed and renewed. When confronted with our test at modern-day Marah and the sometimes-bitter waters of isolation and our online congregations, do we also look to man rather than God for relief?

We have been trained to look to government for intervention. To science and industry for solutions to our concerns. To ourselves to be the heroes and sheroes needed in a crisis. And to faith only when all else fails. However, here in the desperation of our thirst, we will learn to call on the one who is able to save. The one who is able to provide. We will discover that the one who came to free us is enough. The Creator may indeed move through governments, and modern-day rulers may employ the intellect and creativity of the sciences and art. But they are tools at God's disposal and we ourselves are instruments in his hand.

The Israelites were not lost. They were led to the bitter waters of Marah intentionally. The water's purpose was not to punish but to teach. What is the lesson we are learning on the banks of our present condition? What previous ways of being are we now being led to let go of? God did not send Israel to another source of water but challenged them to call on him in the midst of their present condition so he could demonstrate his power to make the bitter sweet.

We do not need to return to Egypt's Nile and our former slavery for refreshment. If we learn to listen to the voice of the Lord and do what is right, if we pay attention to his instructions—love God and neighbor as he commands—then we can know him, not just as the God who saves but also as the one who heals.

9

IN GRIEF AND JOY

Then Job got up and tore his robe and shaved his head [in mourning for the children], and he fell to the ground and worshiped [God]. He said,

> "Naked (without possessions) I came [into this world] from
> my mother's womb,
> And naked I will return there.
> The Lord gave and the Lord has taken away;
> Blessed be the name of the Lord." . . .

So Satan departed from the presence of the Lord and struck Job with loathsome boils and agonizingly painful sores from the sole of his foot to the crown of his head. And Job took a piece of broken pottery with which to scrape himself, and he sat [down] among the ashes (rubbish heaps).

Then his wife said to him, "Do you still cling to your integrity [and your faith and trust in God, without blaming Him]? Curse God and die!" But he said to her, "You speak as one of the [spiritually] foolish women speaks [ignorant and oblivious to God's will]. Shall we indeed accept [only] good from God and not [also] accept adversity and disaster?" In [spite of] all this Job did not sin with [words from] his lips. (Job 1:20-22; 2:7-10)

WENT TO A LARGE urban church growing up, full of families and rich in relationships. One particular family was known by most and loved greatly. Mom served by caring for the babies and young children during worship. It wasn't a paid position or even a formal role. She and her daughters just saw a need and started showing up. Most often they were together—mom and her girls. The three daughters were always well-mannered, gentle, and friendly; their mother was warm and caring. So when one of the girls was tragically killed in a car crash on the way home from a family vacation, the entire church mourned.

I was young and remember being shocked and sad when I heard the news. But I was also curious to see how the mom would deal with such a devastating loss and how the family, now fractured, would go on. It wasn't too long before they returned to church and the eyes of the congregation fell on them. People stared with "I'm so sorry" expressions and, after the worship service, swarmed them with hugs and gentle shoulder pats. I studied mom from a distance. I was relieved but also surprised to see her head unbowed and shoulders that did not sag. Her eyes, while soft, were dry, and her face, though sobered by grief, still held that warm, familiar smile. When I finally had the opportunity to speak with her, she shared that while they were sad to lose their daughter, they accepted that God chose to take her home with him.

I heard people whispering, "It just hasn't hit her yet," and I wondered if that was true. But over the days, weeks, months, and years that followed, her posture remained the same. She continued caring for the babies and toddlers from week to week while wearing a button with a photo of her daughter's smiling face in honor and remembrance.

I thought of Job's story often while watching that mother and was moved and challenged in my own faith. I wondered if I was visited by the tragedy of grief and loss would I, like this mother, be gracious or, like Job, bow down in praise? Or would I stomp and rant and give in to Mrs. Job's suggestion to "curse God and die"?

While grief is a natural response to the loss of a loved one and includes in its course times of anger and anguish, the enemy of our soul is never content with our sorrow but wants to push us ever downward to loss of hope and deep despair. And there is often some well-meaning or evil-intentioned relative or friend available to tempt us into accusing God of wrongdoing or being unfaithful and defaming his character.

Throughout time the question has echoed: why do bad things happen to good people? However, I think the question could also be: why do good things happen to good people? The implication is it's because they are good. The often-overlooked truth, however, is that it's because God is good. Job asks his wife, and perhaps us as well, "Shall we indeed accept only good from God and not also accept adversity and disaster?"

Freed from bondage, Israel rejoiced with singing over God's faithful deliverance from slavery. But a short time later in the wilderness, their dancing turned to moaning and griping and complaining. They quickly forgot about the Lord's goodness and the gift of their newfound freedom. They railed against Moses, their leader—a suitable substitute for yelling at God himself.

When adversity or disaster finds us, the age-old question creeps silently into our minds and hearts again. Why do bad things happen to good people like us? Where is God? But we forget that Jesus said, "No one is [essentially] good [by nature] except God alone" (Mark 10:18). Our perception of good and evil is distorted.

It is because of the LORD's lovingkindness that we are
not consumed,
because His [tender] compassions never fail.

They are new every morning;
Great and beyond measure is Your faithfulness.
(Lamentations 3:22-23)

Job recognized and acknowledged God's consistency.

Naked (without possessions) I came [into this world] from
my mother's womb,
And naked I will return there.
The LORD gave and the LORD has taken away;
Blessed be the name of the LORD. (Job 1:21)

10

IN THE SILENCE

S **ILENCE IS POWERFUL.** It is convicting. It is exposing. It is his.
I have found God's voice to be most piercing, most clear in the silence, in the stillness and calm of solitude.

In the hustle of our everyday lives, we have few moments of silence, few opportunities to stand in the vacuum of noise, few chances to just stop and listen.

For some time now I have set aside one day a week to stop all other activities and prioritize the blank page—to write. Most weeks it is a fight. Warring through the notifications buzzing from my phone. Resisting the endless chatter of the coming and going in my house.

I like the blare of the music and talk spilling from the various speakers in my life, the endless stream of information pouring incessantly from every device. The hum and screech and growl coming from the streets of my city. The barking dogs, the rumble of construction equipment, and the crescendo and swoosh of every car as it approaches, passes by, and then disappears. I like the noise, the sounds, the ever-present distractions of life that my brain can recognize and sort and busy itself with managing.

But it is in the silence that he finds me, exposed and vulnerable. Here I fight to stay open and attentive to his voice and to block out all the other meaningless sound. My body and mind love the city— big, noisy, vibrating with energy—but my soul needs the silence.

> After He had dismissed the crowds, He went up on the mountain by Himself to pray. When it was evening, He was there alone. (Matthew 14:23)

Jesus frequently sought out and found the silence: on the mountain, in the garden, and even while strolling in the night on the waves of the sea. The one who knew all, had all, could do all, contained all since the beginning, left all on the regular to be still and to listen.

> Early in the morning, while it was still dark, Jesus got up, left [the house], and went out to a secluded place. (Mark 1:35)

Some of us have never known God in silence. We met him in the chaos of the everyday or in the noise of calamity or grief. Others found God in the shouts of praise and worship of the church, under loud booming prophesies, clapping hands, or beating drums. The God who whispers is unfamiliar, seems foreign or even threatening. The God who calls me apart and communicates through the ears of my mind and heart can even seem intrusive or overwhelming at first.

So, we often do all we can to avoid the silence. Yet here is where we are disarmed. Here is where we are unmasked and realigned with the divine.

Not long after moving to Atlanta, my husband and I visited the nearby city of Savannah. Savannah is an old city dripping in the history of the plantation South. Sightseeing in the city included a stop at First African Baptist Church, which claims to be the first black Baptist congregation in North America. First Baptist also served as a stop on the Underground Railroad and is said to have housed many runaway slaves during the Civil War. An elderly gentleman was our tour guide through the building and led us eventually to the U-shaped balcony overlooking the sanctuary. I took a seat to rest in the comfort of the red velvet chairs while my husband continued following the elder deacon. I sat in the quiet of the sanctuary, thinking about the many men and women who hid under the floorboards of that room praying to the God who sees.

As I sat there in the silence listening, I began to hear the most amazing sound. The sound of voices singing, rich and warm in the a cappella harmony of black chorus. My heart began to pound and my eyes searched the empty room. I breathed deeply, allowing the Spirit to wash over me. My eyes closed and the melody became a hum in my own throat to a tune I did not know beneath words I had never before heard. After what felt like a long while, I opened my eyes to see the deacon and my husband come into view below me. They continued to talk quietly and I searched their faces for any sign that they too heard the music, were aware of the song. Finding none, I made my way down from the balcony, trying desperately to memorize the tune and the lyrics to the chorus of the song the Spirit had allowed me to hear.

Through the silence I connected not only with the Lord of heaven but also with the souls of the saints who had filled these hallowed pews so long ago. And my heart sang along with them of hope and freedom and joy.

I have met God again and again in the silence of my days when I have made room and come to him with hopeful expectation. When my heart is clear and my mind is at rest, he has met me. In the depth and mystery of silence.

Part Two

DISCOVERING CALL

11

GOD CALLING

Then the LORD came and stood and called as at the

previous times, "Samuel! Samuel!" Then Samuel

answered, "Speak, for Your servant is listening."

1 SAMUEL 3:10

FOR MOST OF US, it doesn't happen all at once but over the course of time. After a series of small but important decisions and some critical turns in the road, we find ourselves on that narrow path, moving away from the crowds and into the quiet of call.

I do not remember a time when anyone specifically spoke to me about a "call" from God. I don't think that was a thing anyone, at that time, ever said to a young black girl. And yet it came nonetheless. A call is a destination, a terminus, a reason for moving forward. We are not just called by God or merely receive a call from God. We are called *to* God. A call is a purpose for being and our first identity.

The ultimate purpose for creation is to glorify God. We are made in the image of the Most High, after God's likeness, in order to reflect

God's splendid excellence in the earth. In him we live, move, and have our being.

> By Him all things were created in heaven and on earth, [things] visible and invisible, . . . all things were created and exist through Him [that is, by His activity] and for Him. (Colossians 1:16)

As early as the womb we begin to sense God drawing us, calling us back to ourselves, the self that is found, known, and understood by the creature only in her connection with the Creator. I began to experience call as this drawing to God. This yearning for God, to know him and to be known, in my late teens. Almost simultaneously, there was an awareness of and desire to pursue the thing for which I was being pursued.

Each one of us carries a distinct divine likeness through which God wants to be revealed to the world. The *imago Dei* is not limited to a physical body. Made in the image of God, we are also made after the nature of the divine—creative, intelligent, compassionate, and kind. God, being love and light in us, is expressed or revealed through the "filters" of our gender, ethnicity, and culture. Through my unique combination of gifts and perspective, I am called out and called forth to respond to the world, the pain and need and breathtaking joy of it. God, through the prism of the Spirit, works in us to refract and disperse that light.

> It is [not your strength, but it is] God who is effectively at work in you, both to will and to work [that is, strengthening, energizing, and creating in you the longing and the ability to fulfill your purpose] for His good pleasure. (Philippians 2:13)

Our individual and specific callings work in harmony with the calling of all others in fulfillment of one overarching purpose: to glorify God. We may not initially fully understand the details of our assignment, but as we move toward him, we move toward it with ever-increasing clarity.

I resist the reference to this call as a burden. A burden implies something heavy that you would like to get rid of but that you are forced to carry or endure. As I yield to the Spirit in response to this call, I, working according to design, am becoming more and more myself. Creativity is awakened and ideas begins to flow. Resources are unlocked and time grows wings. There is energy and insight and laughter and strength. The more we give out, the more we receive, and rest, when it comes, is sweet.

However, along the way we are met with distractions and disappointments and can sometimes become disoriented by the darkness of the world. The burdens we experience are often those we share with others when the suffering we relieve, through love, becomes our own.

Call is the divine whisper inviting us ever forward into the communion and fellowship that comes with surrender. It is never a task required to earn God's love or salvation. It is rather an invitation to enter and share in his work of the redemption of all things. As we move toward that for which we have been created, we find strength and joy. It is life source and life-giving.

I came to know God in the midst of answering call, and along the way I found myself.

12

IMPOSTER SYNDROME

For if anyone thinks he is something [special] when [in fact] he is
nothing [special except in his own eyes], he deceives himself.

GALATIANS 6:3

BIG THINGS. WHAT THAT MEANS VARIES based on the size of the
one doing the assessment and the number of resources at hand.
Moving a five-foot-high pile of wood chips when you're a man with
a backhoe is no big deal. But if you're a girl with a trowel, it becomes
a big thing. Still, I think God most often chooses the girl with the
trowel. In light of this, why do we spend so much time and energy
trying to be "the man" or to acquire the applicable "backhoe"?
Trying to look bigger. Trying to be more. Trying.

God often chooses small, unequipped folks to do big things. He
called Noah to build an ark. Called Solomon to build a temple. Called
Nehemiah to build a wall and a gate and the courage of a people.
Chose David to fight a giant. Called Esther to face a king. Chose
Gideon to lead an army and a teenage Hebrew girl to bear his Son.

When we say yes to this call, to this choosing, the power of heaven is activated on our behalf. Stones and staves and tiny armies become empowered to accomplish God's will. Men and women gain insight and courage, wisdom and knowledge, creativity and strength, and before you know it, they achieve the improbable and unlikely in his name.

Imposter syndrome is "the condition of feeling anxious and not experiencing success internally, despite being high-performing in external, objective ways. With imposter syndrome, a person doesn't feel confident or competent, regardless of what they achieve."[1] Many people, especially women and people of color, report experiencing this. As a recovering perfectionist I sometimes get stuck in the loop of trying. Trying to make it better. Trying to do more. Trying to achieve perfection. And when my outcomes fall short of my perfect plans, as they most often do, I catch myself running the mental clip of my failing on repeat, thinking of all the ways I could have done it better. The things I could have said or the way I should have said it. No matter how well it goes, how much is achieved, I see the misses and shortcomings like bright neon signs flashing to expose my inadequacies to the world.

I hesitate to take on the big. The God-sized plan or project into which he is always inviting me. I want to avoid the task that looks impossible and opt instead for the safe and sure. The things the flesh feels confident to handle. But God calls me out to the deep. To the places where the water is over my head. To do the thing that is too much for the little I have to offer and to make the change practical folks say will never be. God wants to do God-sized things through our fish and our loaves and our bands of tiny men. He wants to take your mistakes and your failings, and my weaknesses and human frailties, and use them to do the impossible so he will get the glory and faith will be increased in the hearts of men.

I am not claiming to be an imposter when I acknowledge my limitations. Instead, I am confessing a truth that gives me access to divine, unlimited power. In the wilderness, stripped of the things that lure me into a false sense of importance and self-deceit, I have learned to rehearse a mantra that quiets my fears and brings clarity: *I have nothing. I can do nothing. I am nothing without him. But with God, I can do all things.*

I whisper it and the noise of my negative loop goes quiet. I recite it and the path ahead becomes clear. My trying gives way to yielding and my mind and soul find rest. God does not choose me because I am perfect or call me for what I possess. He chose me to be a fruit bearer, promised that my fruit would last and that whatever I asked, in his name—for his purpose and glory—the Father would give.

I met God as God, the sovereign, all-powerful one, in the wilderness of my lack and imperfections. And I found him to be more than enough.

13

I AM THE WAY

T HERE'S SOMETHING UNSETTLING about a one-way ticket. It's a beginning without a prearranged end, a departure without a return. I don't like one-way tickets. I'm not comfortable with open-ended tales. I want to know where we're going, how and when we'll get there, and the means of transportation. I want to know the details, perhaps most important of which is how and when we will get back.

Following Jesus is a one-way ticket. No one returns back to the exact point of departure. As the old spiritual says, "Every round goes higher, higher." When Jesus said, "Follow me" to his disciples, I imagine they may have had a few questions along the way. Where are we going, Jesus? How much will it cost? How long will it take to get there? Where will we sleep? Is it safe?

Perhaps not at first. At first, we are just thrilled to be chosen. To be among the few. Excitement produces compliance, and we quickly line up and start moving. But before long we begin straining our necks to see around the person in front of us. Our eyes dart with concern at the roads passed on our left and right but not chosen. Worst of all, we look behind us at the faces and places now fading into the distance and struggle to push down the nagging questions that fight for attention in our minds. *Did I make a mistake choosing to follow this leader? Respond too quickly to the invitation? Step out too soon or reflect inadequately on this call?* Our steps, once quick and light, become increasingly heavy and slow, resulting in our falling out of step with the Master and leaving us further and further behind.

As young children, toddlers, we are fine traveling without a destination. We walk or are carried to car seats, get strapped in to our back-of-the-car designated seating area, and ride. We may complain about being hot or cold, hungry, tired, or wet, but never about where we are going or our lack of input in the travel destination. We trust that mom or dad, older sibling or sitter, will protect us and provide what is needed. We don't need to know all the details. We just need to know the person.

Israel was fine keeping step on their way out of Egypt and followed closely while Pharoah's army was closing in behind. But once the chariot wheels disappeared under the waves and the city of bondage fell from view, they started forming questions, having doubts, and second-guessing their decisions and their leader.

> And He said to them, "Follow Me [as My disciples, accepting Me
> as your Master and Teacher and walking the same path of life
> that I walk], and I will make you fishers of men." (Matthew 4:19)

The invitation from Jesus is a simple one. Follow me. Walk on the path I've chosen. Choose my route over your own. Walk the way I'm walking—match my gait and my pace. When you are tempted to lag behind or run ahead, don't. Wait for me. Walk with me. Follow me. Walk toward the destination I have chosen, even when you don't understand. Even when you disagree. Follow me into the unfamiliar or foreign, through the discomfort and the fear.

Some years ago I was introduced to the sacred beauty of labyrinths. The labyrinth is a winding path within a circle. Through twists and turns, each walker steadily makes her way toward an opening in the center and then back out again, never crossing the same steps twice. It is important to enter the labyrinth alone and to travel at your own pace. Along the way you may encounter other travelers, but their journey is not yours. Though your paths may appear very close, they will never be the same. You walk and you pray. You breathe and reflect and fight the temptation that returns again and again, when it feels like you are wandering on a road to nowhere, to give up and walk away.

If you instead persist, somewhere along the way the need for control and the anxious searching to see how close you are to the end falls away and you just enjoy the stroll. Yielded to the calm that is found in the rhythm of our footsteps, you can discover and be renewed by the peace that waits in the beauty of the present moment. You can remember what it is to trust and believe and simply hope again in him.

Where we exit the labyrinth is never the same place that we started. And while all the noise and chaos and challenge of the outside world may still be there, perhaps we are just a little better prepared to handle it.

"Follow me," he says, "on this one-way journey called discipleship—my way, at my pace, to my destination—and I will make you, change you, form you, transform you into fishers of men."

14

SUBMERSION IS SUBMISSION

"You are My Son, My Beloved,
in You I am well-pleased and delighted!"

LUKE 3:22

BEFORE JESUS ENTERED THE WILDERNESS, perhaps in preparation for it, there is a brief accounting by Luke in 3:21-22 of his baptism. There are three things to note about this baptism. It was public. Jesus was praying. And the Holy Spirit—or the Holy Ghost, as some would say in more charismatic circles—was poured out.

Baptism is an act of submission, a public declaration, that you are yielding your life to the will of the divine. It is the forgetting and letting go of what was before. Before this day, before this moment in time, before this submersion into the grave of the water. Jesus was thirty years old at his baptism. He had lived thirty years of a lifetime. He had relationships and a trade, a family and a faith. He had a community and a way of doing and being in the world. However, on this day, perhaps before family and friends and strangers, he was giving all that up, yielding over his present reality to become his past.

To be fair, Jesus was never an ordinary child. After all, a choir of angels appeared singing to announce his birth. Rich scientists showed up with gifts to worship him as a toddler, and by the age of twelve he was expounding on the Scripture in the temple before an audience of scholars. He was never ordinary, but he was a man and, as the Bible says, acquainted with grief. He had lived long enough to have laughed and cried, to have gained friends and favor, and now, in the knowledge of all that was and would be, to suffer loss. But he was willing, before the multitude and by the hands of one less worthy, to give himself over to the Father's will. The surrender of his life began not on a cross on a hill but in a river called Jordan.

In like manner, my wilderness did not begin on a highway headed south to Georgia but years before at a fork in the road in the woods.

Just into our thirties, my husband and I had left our safe jobs with vacation pay and health benefits to raise our three children and start a nonprofit organization. We were serving in our church. He had been recently licensed as a minister and was preaching; I was leading the children's choir. Together we led the youth. We both worked part time at the little Christian school in our neighborhood, but I sensed God inviting us into deeper waters.

At the invitation of a couple we had recently met, my husband and I attended a weekend retreat at a campground near the mountains in Pennsylvania. At some point I wandered off for a quiet walk by myself. Having no desire to get lost in exploration, I stayed to the wide gravel path enjoying the cool of the shade, the sound of the birds, and the peeks of sunshine through the leaves. Before too long, though, I could see I was headed toward a point where my nice neat path branched off in two distinctly different directions. I slowed my pace before coming to a stop at the fork.

There were no signs or markers. Nothing to distinguish one option over the other. I hesitated, unsure which way to go, concerned about getting lost and being able to find my way back to the campground. It was then that Spirit began to whisper.

Donna, are you willing to be made poor so that others might be made rich?

I felt my heart begin to beat faster and my breathing become shallow the way it does when you become aware of being in the presence of the Most High God. I remained still and silent, and for a time it felt as if time stood still.

I'm giving you a choice, he said. *You can continue down a road of safety and comfort or you can choose the path I am calling you to.*

There were no details offered about this other path. No descriptions, disclaimers, or specifics of any kind. It was simply an invitation, a "Follow me" and an outstretched hand.

Are you willing to become poor so that others can be made rich?

The question hung suspended in the space around me between the sunlight and the shade, between the sound and the silence. In that moment that stretched out seemingly forever, I was aware of two things. First, that his words were true. He was giving me a real choice, not a command. I had always been a rule follower. If he had said, "Do this," I would have said, "Yes, Lord," in obedience. But he was asking for something more from me, something bigger than blind obedience. He was asking for trust. Trust in him and in his love for me.

The second thing I was certain of was that the poverty he spoke of on the path toward call was real, not figurative. I stood in that moment for a period of time that felt like forever before at last venturing a step forward, with my body and spirit, toward the path that veered to the right. I felt the tears fall as I whispered an audible, "Yes, Lord, I'm willing."

I stepped into the Jordan consenting and let the waters of his will cover me. That is the baptism we are called to. *Yes*, is the prayer that is prayed. Submission opens the heavens and allows the Holy Ghost to descend, poured out in preparation for new life and for the wilderness to come.

15

HUNGRY IN THE FAR COUNTRY

"Behold, the days are coming," says the Lord God,

"When I will send hunger over the land,

Not hunger for bread or a thirst for water,

But rather [a hunger] for hearing the words of the Lord."

AMOS 8:11

HERE IS AN ACCOUNT IN LUKE 15 WHERE Jesus is teaching about a lost sheep, a lost coin, and a lost son. The consecutive parables appear to highlight the similar responses to the recovery of lost items or people, emphasizing the joy and celebration when they are found. As I was thinking about this recently, I was struck by the differences between the things lost.

The sheep is likely lost because sheep, unrestrained, will wander. While focused on grazing, they lose sight of the flock and the shepherd. They do not have a strong sense of direction and can struggle to find the fold even when it is in sight. They do not wander with intention but rather as a result of their genuine weaknesses.

Then there is the coin. The coin, an inanimate object, does not lose itself but instead is misplaced or lost by the owner. It does not willfully roll away or slide itself under a rug or piece of furniture. No, the coin is lost by someone who then rejoices greatly with friends and neighbors when it is later found.

Finally, there is the lost son. He is not lost because he got confused and innocently wandered away. He is not a child who was mistakenly left at the church or school by his busy and distracted parents (hypothetically speaking, of course, not at all a confession of any kind!). No, the son becomes lost by his own will. Perhaps he'd become bored in his assigned role or dissatisfied with his lifestyle. Maybe he was disappointed at being the younger son in a system that favored the elder, or frustrated and angry with how things were run at his father's house, or let down by an unfair system that did not permit him consideration for leadership or meaningful participation. Whatever the reasoning, the son gathered his things and demanded his portion of his inheritance and walked deliberately away, traveling to a distant "far country."

The thing about anger, disappointment, righteous indignation, or even rebellion is that they all eventually take a back seat to hunger. The far country, for all its glitz and sugary excitement, cannot sustain us. Like cotton candy, it is bright and colorful and delightful to the senses for a season. But its promises, like those calories, are empty and leave us unsatisfied. Relationships in the far country can be numerous but connection rare, and in the wave of real-life challenge they often fade or disappear. Without warning and sooner than we could have imagined, our resources are spent and we discover ourselves alone in the midst of a social, emotional, or even literal famine.

Hungry I come to you, for I know you satisfy.[1]

It begins as an ache. A nudge from inside us, reminding us of something forgotten that still we need. We try to ignore it, distract ourselves with sleep or a scroll, but hunger unanswered moves from ache to grumble then quickly swells to a roar. So we construct a plan and put it in motion, meant to satisfy the yearning and drown out the growing noise. But our plans have a way of taking us farther and farther off course, and before long we are knee-deep in the filth and stink of the formerly forbidden, desperately longing for that which previously we would not have considered. We are hungry.

It is here, with God's grace, we acknowledge that what began as an exciting quest into freedom has spiraled into something else. We have been marching in circles in the wilderness. We, like the prodigal, got lost. But what makes the son lost? It is not because he doesn't know his way home, for once he made the decision to go, he was able to get there. Sometimes people have to come looking for us. At other times we need to recover ourselves.

Here, covered in the mud of our misery, the Spirit can meet us and we can remember what is true. We are hungry, but we have a home where even the angelic servants of our Father are cared for and blessed with more than enough. We can make a decision to return to the arms and home of our Father, not because we are deserving but because he is good.

Jesus concludes his teaching with the unfortunate reality that not everyone in the Father's house will be happy to see us or ready to offer an embrace. Some siblings will be just as we left them: unkind, unwelcoming, and unreflective of the Father's love. But our time in the far country has changed us and led us to a hard truth previously unknown. There is room for us both in the family of the Father, and a robe, ring, and banquet of grace is ours should we choose it when we get home.

16

TAKE COURAGE

TIRED OF SITTING INSIDE ALL DAY, I decided to venture out on a walk through the neighborhood. Having recently returned to the community, I was having trouble adjusting to being in a familiar place with a foreign feel. Blocks and porches now empty and strangely silent were missing the noise and laughter of the children I once knew, the whiz of bikes, the bark of dogs, and the warm greetings of neighbors. The neighborhood was still and quiet, like a movie paused on the screen. It seemed that, like me, it was waiting, hoping, ready for the next important thing to begin.

Rounding the corner, I came to a conclusion. This stillness, this waiting, is an exercise in patience. A test of our resolve to trust and wait on him. Courage is not something that takes over in the height of the emotion of the moment, but rather, like faith, it is a conscious choice we must make every day. And despite my love for the Marvel franchise, I have learned that courage is not relegated to spandex-clad heroes who fell victim to spider venom or a lab experiment or a strange mutation. It is most noticeable in the words and actions of ordinary men and women who, being chosen, must choose to act on what they hope for and fight for what they do not yet see.

It also takes courage to wait when it seems like the crowd is thinning or rushing on ahead. To be still when everything in you wants to run. It requires courage to mark time for what feels like forever in the dust of real disappointment and not give in to cynicism or unbelief.

I often think about Joshua and the priests and armies of Israel marching for days around the walls of the city of Jericho.

> But Joshua commanded the people, "You shall not shout [the battle cry] nor let your voice be heard nor let a word come out of your mouth, until the day I tell you to shout. Then you shall shout!" (Joshua 6:10)

How frustrating it must have felt by the fourth day, walking in circles in silence. Nothing but the sound of the ram's horn and marching feet. Joshua gave instructions for each day, and the people walked without knowing what the end of their obedience would bring. They kept walking despite how foolish they may have felt. They walked again on the next day even though there was no visible sign of change. They walked even though the instructions made no sense. Their efforts seemed futile. Their experience suggested it was pointless, because when had this kind of marching ever opened city gates or brought down stone walls?

Three times in the beginning of the book God challenged Joshua to be strong and courageous. It would take courage to cross over the waters of the Jordan from the desert life the people had come to know and enter the freedom of the Promised Land. It would take courage to trust in alliances with seemingly powerless people, like the women who lived on the margins and made their living in the shadow of the city walls. And it would take courage to follow God's instructions, resisting the temptation to override them with a "better idea" or the sound of their own voices.

I think about the feet that marched around the walls of the city of Jericho like those that trekked through the streets of Montgomery to protest a racist bus system. Feet that marched over Selma's Edmund Pettus Bridge. Feet that marched for women's suffrage in Washington, voting rights in Alabama, and around the world to affirm the value of black lives. It's courageous to stand in full armor, weapon in hand, but not to raise it. To hold your position while the enemy closes in. Yet God promises good to those who have the courage to wait. Renewed strength and increased endurance to those who trust in him.

Faith is an act of courage and serves as the fuel that propels us forward into change, to believe that things and people can be different after what looks like years of nothing but the same. Yet without faith it is impossible to please God.

Now it calls us to hope again with expectation for that thing in the distance, not quite yet in view. To once again step out into what looks like empty air, possessing nothing but sure of the provision that's on the way.

I met God on the streets of a forgotten little neighborhood. He was in the faces of children and the stories of seniors, some of whom have now passed on. So I believe that now, even in the strange and quiet, his promises will again become new and in his timing his people will shout.

19

IN FAITH OR OBEDIENCE

R ECENTLY I'VE BEEN WONDERING, is humankind better suited for the garden or the wilderness? It would seem that a garden is a more desirable home. A place where we can be fed and watered and enjoy a carpet of soft grass and the cool of shade. But the garden is also forested with all manner of trees, some of which present deadly temptations.

From the beginning we have been confronted with temptation. Confusing knowledge for freedom, we disdain our childlike innocence and opt instead for the often idolatrous knowing of good and evil. To decide for ourselves. To choose our own way. To know. To be like the Most High God.

But just as was true for our elder siblings Adam and Eve, this knowing does not produce the satisfaction we hope for or the contentment we crave. Rather, our knowing often results in new and unexpected fears. We say we seek to know in order to understand. But more often, our knowing is about our desire for control of what is or may be. The provisions and safety and beauty of the garden are not enough for our grasping appetites. It is not enough to be made in the image, to look like or reflect the beauty of the Most High. It is not enough to be filled with and to know the presence and comfort of the Spirit. It is not enough for us to bear the name, be adopted or grafted in as heirs. We want the autonomy and sovereignty of Almighty God.

From the beginning, the garden has been a call to obedience, which Jesus said is the demonstration of reverent love. To walk in obedience is to choose to trust the one who is guiding despite what I think or feel. The lushness of the garden—the provision of every earthly need—is an expression of love.

Yet there, surrounded by fruit trees and berries, nuts, herbs, and leafy greens, we become restless. We forget our need for God. We start believing that a gift is earned, lovingkindness deserved, and obedience an oppressive, outdated expectation. When there's money in the account, the kids are doing well, and we are praised as the best or the brightest of the month, we wink at the face in the mirror and think, "Well done, you!" We forget the prayers we prayed and the faithfulness of the one who answered.

Just hearing the word *obey* can raise feelings of resentment and a knee-jerk response to resist. It is a concept we associate with pets and young children who need to be controlled. So we rebel to exert our independence, our autonomy, our maturity. Most often in America we are socialized to resist, to declare our freedom. Then we hear the words of Jesus gently coaxing, "If you [really] love me, you will keep and obey My commandments" (John 14:15).

Obedience is the faithful response to an unconditional love. It is a decision we must make every day. It is the willing demonstration of my faith in the one who knows me and loves me and my belief that he has planned the best for me. It is also the perpetual acknowledgment of my weakness and true dependence on him. The strange thing is, when I acknowledge my lack of knowledge or power, it often opens the floodgate of divine resource to provide me with whatever is necessary to complete the task he has assigned to me, the thing he has instructed me to do. When I acknowledge his lordship, I am entrusted with greater leadership and responsibility. When I look past my desires and surrender my will to his as an expression of love, God responds with greater and greater demonstrations of his power and favor in my life.

> God is not a man, that He should lie,
> Nor a son of man, that He should repent.
> Has He said, and will He not do it?
> Or has He spoken and will He not make it good and fulfill it?
>   (Numbers 23:19)

Obedience keeps the weight of responsibility for outcomes on God. I am not asked to fulfill his promises. I am not stressed with the task of saving anyone or even conforming myself to the image of Christ. That is his work. Those are his promises. I am asked only to seek him and to respond to his instruction with "Yes, Lord." But sometimes I forget and get off track. Sometimes I choose my own way, thinking I know better. Sometimes I say, "No," or "Not now," and march defiantly in the opposite direction. Sometimes I choose the one forbidden tree.

Periodically, as individuals or collectively in our local churches, we are led away from the comfort and the certainty of the garden into the unknown and the challenge that is wilderness. Here the trees are sparse and the path less defined. We get disoriented and confused and reacquainted with thirst. When our legs grow weary and our bellies growl, we begin to remember the one our soul desires. We stop stomping away and turn back toward him. We fall to our knees and ask for help. We admit our hunger and confess our thirst, abandon our self-made golden calves and pause to wait for his instructions. He finds us in the harshness of the desert, just as he did in the garden because, thankfully, he is Lord in the wilderness too.

18

PEACE OUT

"THAT'S WHY I LEFT THE CHURCH."

It has become a common phrase that sometimes follows a painful story of personal rejection or abuse. More often, however, it is a general declaration of a decision to step away from the church as an institution or a lifestyle or sometimes even from faith altogether.

Occasionally I find myself doubting the stated reason that precedes it. I wonder if sometimes we walk away from church for the same reason we leave jobs, families, marriages, or neighborhoods. Perhaps sometimes we leave when it becomes easier to go than to stay. When we identify more with what's outside the circle than within. When we're done.

> As a result of this many of His disciples abandoned Him, and no longer walked with Him. So Jesus said to the twelve [disciples], "You do not want to leave too, do you?" (John 6:66-67)

I met God in an all-black, all-Baptist, mostly Democrat, big-city church on the East Coast. While it appeared to me, as a child, that we had most things in common as a congregation, an adult lens has allowed me to realize our many differences as well. We were poor, working class, and middle class. Gay and straight. Intergenerational. Homeowners and renters, public school and private, PhDs and GEDs. An assortment of folks worshiping together to classical music and gospel, pipe organs and drums.

Diversity is part of God's design for the universe, as evidenced by the number of planets in various sizes and climates. An assortment of insects. A rainbow of colors. An endless variety of animals and birds and flowers. And while the snowflakes are all white, no two patterns are exactly the same. Diverse community is also God's design for spiritual growth and sharing the gospel. We are different by design. And difference, with intentionality, can result in harmony.

However, sometimes, amid the challenges of living, bands become factions. Demands are made for a "unity" that requires a unison—everyone speaking with one voice—in agreement with or in surrender to a dominant point of view.

In recent years it seems our ability to "disagree without being disagreeable" has waned. Patience and longsuffering have been abandoned. And some, mistaking lack of conflict for shalom, choose silence or absence over truth in love. So when we cannot convince or be convinced, cannot bear or will not bear with, do not understand or feel misunderstood, we walk away. We avoid. We disengage. We abandon. We dis-member ourselves from the body.

My childhood congregation was large enough to include a variety of people and large enough to hold bands of similarity within tribes of difference. Real community, especially if it includes difference, requires commitment. Placing a group of people together in the same space does not make it a community. Shared trauma may create bonds, but it doesn't make family. Shared joy may create pleasant memories, but it doesn't ensure a lasting connection. Many disciples walked away from Jesus when the ask became too much. When they felt his words were offensive or when the message became hard to understand.

Similarly, when the conflict feels too big for us or the learning curve is too steep or the other person's point of view is too confusing, offensive, or wrongheaded, we are tempted to follow the crowd out the door. But the Word and Spirit of God confront us as Jesus did the Twelve: "Do you also want to walk away?"

Jesus is not a social media platform that we safely "follow" from an anonymous distance, nor is the church an electronic device we use to access him. We are called to share the good news of God's grace and love beyond words, through the model of relationships. We are called to be and make disciples in the context of diverse community. But we can only live in that dissonance with an unwavering faith in Jesus as Lord.

Now, of course, not every particular congregation is a healthy place to be. And sometimes it is the essence of wisdom to pull aside and reconsider our position or recalculate a route. Still, when we think deeply about the reasons we left or desire to leave, we must acknowledge that not all of us have been abused or rejected. Prayerful reflection may reveal that some of us leave because we reject discomfort. We resist accountability. We hate conflict. We lack courage.

Peter responds to Jesus' question with his own. "Lord, to whom shall we go?"

Our answer to that question may determine whether we stay or walk away. Where do you find your identity and belonging? If there is any person or group or organization or party with whom I more greatly identify than him, it may seem like I have a choice, especially on the hard days. But the truth is that Christ alone is our peace. He alone has the words of eternal life. He is the one in whom we live, move, and have our being. And he has promised his presence when we come together in his name.

19

"DO YOU LOVE ME?"

MY LOVE LANGUAGE IS ACTS OF KINDNESS. As a result, what often shows up as busyness is me trying to express love to a family member or friend, my church or my community. Recently I realized that this is also how I express my love to God. I join the worship team. I lead a committee or board. I plan the event, write the letter, make the time in my busy day for the unexpected lunch, dinner, or coffee or to take one more call. It's the least I can do, I think to myself, for the one who has done so much for me. Hard work and multitasking? No problem, Lord. If anything, it's prolonged stillness I find challenging.

The point of knowing love languages, however, is not just to affirm how I want to be loved and express love but also to discover how to best love others. So sometimes, despite my flurry of activity, I hear him whisper in the quiet of my heart, *Donna, do you love me?*

Immediately I quip, like Peter, "Lord, you know I love you!" I scrunch my face into a "How could you ask that?" expression.

Another question quickly follows the first. *More than these?* This time I pause to consider. More than what?

When Jesus posed the question to Peter, some believe he was asking, "More than these other men?" I wonder, though, if he's asking me something deeper. Do you love me more than what I am asking you to give up? Do you love me more than the things you believe you have a right to? More than the things that make you comfortable? That make you seen? That make you feel safe and in control? *Donna, do you love me more than these?*

Actually, it would be easier if he just asked us about our pastimes or possessions. The job or the naps or the favorite food or toy. It gets personal when he probes past the petty and the simple. Into the locked doors and secret drawers of our hearts.

Do you love me more than your right to your "righteous" anger? More than having your way to do what you've always done or executing your well-thought-out plans? Do you love me more than your favorite people or your reputation? More than your comfort or your imagined future or even more than life itself?

Some of us have marched out of our past life carrying all the stuff we accumulated in our bondage. We hold tight to the possessions in our hands, the old life values, and the attitudes of our hearts. We trudge through the desert of now, sweating under the enormous weight of the past, believing we can carry all that we were, all that we had, all that we knew into the next and not yet. It's awkward and exhausting, but how could we not bring it? It's backbreaking. But you never know what you might need.

Do you love Me more than these? (John 21:15)

My husband and I have moved across the country twice and purposed each time to rid ourselves of the unneeded and unnecessary. We failed. Worse the second time than the first. Somehow the promise to bring only clothes and bedroom furniture grew into us packing out a trailer, two cars, and an RV. We were moving to a different climate and a home with far less space. But we loaded the boxes just the same.

When Jesus called Peter and his brother Andrew (Matthew 4:18-20), they were working as fishermen by the Sea of Galilee. At Jesus' invitation they immediately left their nets and gear and followed him to become his disciples. Later it seems that Peter may not have abandoned the old job but just put his fishing tools in storage, because despite two post-resurrection appearances by Jesus, he's back to his old job fishing. Jesus asks the question, "Simon, son of John, do you love me more than these?" Jesus' question speaks to the one thing that matters when we are attempting to move forward in our walk, in our call, or into the next phase of life: our steadfast love for him.

God in Christ Jesus uses all of the love languages to demonstrate his love for us and tells us directly how he wants to be loved—through our obedience and love for others. But often we have other stuff in our hands and other ideas about how we want to love him.

"Do you love *me*?" he asks, with an emphasis on the last pronoun. Do you love me or the things I am offering? Do you love me or the protection I provide? Do you love me or your status in your organization, in the church, on the board, or in the community? Do you love me or the pleasure of crossing me off your daily to-do list?

The love we have for him when we are standing still in the silence, hands and pockets empty, is what we will need to move ourselves and the church into the promised kingdom that lies ahead.

20

FOR THE PRIZE

Do you not know that in a race all the runners run [their very best to win], but only one receives the prize? Run [your race] in such a way that you may seize the prize and make it yours! Now every athlete who [goes into training and] competes in the games is disciplined and exercises self-control in all things. They do it to win a crown that withers, but we [do it to receive] an imperishable [crown that cannot wither]. Therefore, I do not run without a definite goal; I do not flail around like one beating the air [just shadow boxing]. But [like a boxer] I strictly discipline my body and make it my slave, so that, after I have preached [the gospel] to others,

I myself will not somehow be disqualified [as unfit for service].

1 CORINTHIANS 9:24-27

MY HUSBAND AND I LOVE to travel and have planned to make it a highlight of our golden years (whenever those come). And since we are opposites in everything, we have of course had "the destination versus the journey" debate many times. For me, it's definitely about where we're going, the final stop, and all that we will see and experience once we get there. The time between departure and arrival used to be my greatest frustration. For Leroy, it's all about the trip, the open road or skies and the path we travel along the way.

Fortunately, over the years, we have found ourselves moving closer and closer to one another on this. I have learned that, while God certainly has an outcome in mind, he is also definitely at work in the process. And I believe Leroy has discovered that a scenic route may be pleasant for a time but when the gas is low and your feet get tired, it helps a lot to know how much farther you have to go and where exactly you will land.

I have also discovered that just because you're wandering it doesn't mean you are lost. Israel wandered for forty years in their wilderness. They were not lost. They were in process. God had given them a specific destination and they were on course. He just didn't attach it to a timeline. I've learned that although his promises "are yes and amen," they take as long as they take to get there because they, or you, do not arrive until you are ready.

However, sometimes we get distracted by the journey and lose sight of our desired end. We're unprepared for the change of weather. We haven't packed the correct shoes. We didn't pace ourselves for the length of the trip or the steepness of the climb, and before you know it, we're running low on time, on money, or on strength. We're driving in circles or have wandered off course. We spent money preparing for intense heat only to find ourselves knee-deep in snow.

A few months after a recent move, I found myself running low on hope and on energy and on time. The change in location had disoriented me. I'd lost sight of where I was and had been headed. Furthermore, I had forgotten why. I was moving my feet and pumping my arms as fast as I could without any sense of where I was going. Then I came across Paul's words to the church at Corinth, a reprimand about why we run. To win. The Spirit challenged me and I wrote these words in my journal: "Run your race with a mind to win! You are not just out for a jog!"

I paused and considered. Was I running without a goal? On a trip with no clear destination in sight? Paul's goal was to share the gospel and see as many people come to faith in Christ as possible. It was clear and he was focused. I felt lost, not because I didn't know where I was but because I'd lost sight of where I was going. I had lots of activity, moving around and clocking miles. But it had become meaningless motion just leaving me breathless.

I stopped and took time to consider. What was my mission? What was my unique goal? In the stillness of that moment, I remembered. I exist to know and glorify God, and I do that uniquely through the development of leaders. The location may have changed. The specific roles I fill may be different. But the call is consistent. The destination is sure.

We are not just out for a joy ride. We are going somewhere, and we need to plan accordingly, to keep up with our training and stay prepared for all segments of the trip. If we can be faithful and avoid, as Paul warned, "disqualification," by God's grace we will get to the end of this thing. The prize of his high calling. It will happen when we have been made ready and not one step, day, or mile ahead of his appointed time.

Part Three

FACING FEAR

21

LORD OF THE DARKNESS

DON'T REMEMBER BEING AFRAID of the dark as a child. Perhaps because in the heart of the city, with its streetlights and stoplights, cop lights and neon signs, true darkness can be hard to find. I slept by the window in my tiny bedroom, and through the slats of my window blinds crept the light of my neighbors' homes, the glow from a nearby streetlight, and sometimes, if I squinted, the faint dots of distant stars. The darkness of my room was more like charcoal shadow and varying shades of gray.

But away from the familiar, the darkness feels different. I have often asked the question on late-night road trips, after long stretches of empty highway or while winding along dark back roads, why would anyone choose to live outside the safety of a crowded city, in the barren, scary silence of the woods? Where does that desire even come from? What do you do without the frequent hum of passing buses, the occasional raised voices of passing neighbors, or the screaming rise and fall of a siren in the distance?

Of course, it is not the darkness itself we fear. Darkness is merely the absence of light. We know our closets and the clothes inside them remain the same when we close the doors and turn off the switch. Shirts and shoes do not magically take breath and become living beings as we imagined when we were children. No, it is the unknown we're afraid of. The unclear or indistinct causes us to pause or draw back in fear. So the suburbanite or country kid fears the big, bad city and the city kid dreads the rustle and snapping sounds of the woods.

Darkness can also represent the absence of sufficient information. The feeling of being disoriented, lost, or otherwise out of control. Darkness can be any space away from my comfort zones that leaves me feeling unsafe, confused, or unsure. We generally don't like darkness, whether we can see with our natural eyes or not. We often do everything in our power to avoid it, because in this space, whether our fear is real or imagined, we find ourselves living on high alert, bodies and minds ready to confront the coming threat.

Some years ago my family and I took a vacation. We rented an RV, packed up the kids and bikes, and headed away from Atlanta through the state of Florida and out across the long bridges of the Florida Keys. We set up camp in a beautiful RV campground right along the coast not far from the southernmost point. We arrived during the day and explored the campground in the bright comfort of the afternoon sun. We roasted marshmallows by the warm glow of a campfire at night despite the summer heat.

Near the front end of our camper was a wooden dock that led out to the water by a short pier. I suppose some people used such things for fishing or tanning. I did not, but I enjoyed standing and looking out at the ripples of the water during the day and the distant lights of the city off to the north at night.

One night, after the kids were in bed, I ventured out onto the pier alone, enjoying the warm breeze and soothing sound of the water lapping against the wood. I stood facing the city lights with my back deliberately turned against the dark southern sky. However, before too long I felt prompted by the Spirit to turn to the south. To look with intention into the darkness. It was late and the night was cloudy and starless. The blackness of the sky met the darkness of the water almost seamlessly. I felt my muscles stiffen and the pace of my breathing increase. I squinted into the distance and tried in vain to see. The sound of the wind seemed louder and I noticed what felt like the slight movement of the pier beneath my feet. What was I doing here, away from the safe familiarity of the city? I steadied myself, preparing to head back to the campsite as the darkness seemed to close in around me.

But this was the same pier I had stood on with confidence in the afternoon sunlight. The same sky, once white with clouds, was still over my head. The Spirit of the Lord was inviting me to stay. I remembered the words of David:

> Even the darkness is not dark to You and conceals nothing
> from You,
> But the night shines as bright as the day;
> Darkness and light are alike to You. (Psalm 139:12)

God was not afraid of the dark. He strolled along the floor of the ocean, seeing every rock and fish at midnight, just as if it were noonday. God is not afraid of the unfamiliar places in my life or the not-so-distant future, though it may be out of my line of sight or control. God is not intimidated by the things I am afraid of. He is sovereign over the things I cannot prepare for or foresee. It is okay to move forward without all the answers. Our trust is in an all-wise, all-seeing, all-knowing God.

I stood on that pier until the trembling left my body. I stood still until I again knew that he was God. Until the howl in my ears was just a breeze off the water and the darkness over my head was just the sky.

22

FLATS HAPPEN

A **WHILE BACK MY HUSBAND BOUGHT** his first electric bike. It was a Jetson—small, compact, foldable. I'm not sure what prompted this purchase, but it appeared fairly harmless, so I gave it little thought. I was, however, intrigued by one thing. On the side of the kidney-shaped box that housed the battery were the words *Flats Happen*. I wasn't sure if this was meant to be a warning concerning the bike or a reason for having one. Or perhaps a general commentary on life in general. I lean toward the latter.

You're riding down the road on your way to somewhere minding your own business and *bam*, there's a pop and a hiss and then the plop, plop, plop of a now floppy, deflated tire, and you make your way to the side of the road. It's never convenient or expected and never what you want to deal with. It just is. Flats happen. It's not a reason to give up on riding or driving and return to the former days of horse and buggy. We simply fix it and move on.

A flat is more than a flat only when we are unprepared. When we have just enough time to get to that possibly life-changing interview. When we realize we never repaired or replaced the spare. When we're alone on a dark road just after canceling the roadside assistance feature of our insurance policy to save a little cash. It's then that a flat becomes a potential crisis.

On the road from former to next, flats happen. When they do, sometimes we are tempted to return to the former things. A way of life that did not serve us then and does not fit us now but is familiar. A way of thinking that does not account for the fullness of God or our present resurrected reality. We stumble or take a wrong turn, and an accusatory finger appears pointed in our direction.

"See?" it says. "This is what happens when you don't follow the rules. You messed up and now what? Just go back to the old way. It wasn't perfect, but at least you knew what to expect."

If the terrain is new or unfamiliar, insecurity interprets every obstacle or setback as proof of a navigational error. It whispers, "Just go back to the law. Go back to tradition. Go back to the tried and untrue." Better to opt for familiar bondage than to risk all for an unfamiliar freedom. But in Paul's letter to the Galatian believers, he urges a wavering church to resist the temptation to return to the bondage of the law, a faith of their own making with rules set and managed by their own will and control.

> Keep standing firm and do not be subject again to a yoke of slavery [which you once removed]. (Galatians 5:1)

He is urging a persecuted, oppressed people to "stand fast." Despite the unexpected crisis, stand unyieldingly in your liberty, in the freedom God used to make you free. Plant your feet and maintain your position. Lean into your forward progress. It's easier to look back, to slide back into old ways of thinking and believing. To look at the challenges that remain in this present moment as reasons to retreat. Just as we are poised for change and growth, we feel pressure to shrink. Our stumbles become excuses to be silent. Missteps seem reasons for retreat. But instead, our brother Paul tells us, "do not be subject again to a yoke of slavery." Instead, pull over to the side of the road and change the tire. It's a crisis only if we are unprepared.

The weight of manufacturing our own salvation or righteousness is a yoke too heavy for us to bear. We are prone to falter, and sometimes our best laid plans fall flat. However, persecution is not a reason to return to the old ways of the law.

Sometime after that original purchase, my husband decided to upgrade his bike. He bought a bigger, heavier model with a longer battery life and began to venture out on longer and longer rides. Eventually, the inevitable happened. While a good distance from home enjoying his ride, he suddenly felt his wheel bumping roughly on the asphalt. He didn't have a spare tire hanging around his neck nor the tools to make a repair. He was annoyed but he did the only thing he could do. He got off the bike, made a call, and waited for help.

We are free from the lies of inferiority. Free from the need to earn our place. Free to bring our whole selves into the room. To stand in the light, on the platform, before the throne as a beautiful, God-made creation, without fear. And we are free to make mistakes and to fail and try again, because on this trek from earth to glory, flats happen.

23

PRESSING ON

This is what the LORD says,

> He who makes a way through the sea
> And a path through the mighty waters,
>
> He who brings out the chariot and the horse,
> The army and the mighty warrior,
> (They will lie down together, they will not rise again;
> They have been extinguished, they have been put out like
>   a lamp's wick):
>
> "Do not remember the former things,
> Or ponder the things of the past." (Isaiah 43:16-18)

The waters closed and the life we knew immediately fell into memory. We turned our backs on what was and marched, sang, danced our way forward, reveling in the joy. Sometime later, the sun hung low over the horizon and the tambourines fell silent. All we could hear was the muffled swish of sandals dredging through the dust of our new temporary home, the wilderness.

THERE'S ALWAYS THAT MOMENT when the noise of excitement gives way to settled quiet. When joyful smiles and jubilant laughter fade into the nervous titters of, *now what?* Anyone who has left a long-done relationship or a job or a childhood home has known that feeling, felt that exhilaration of newfound freedom melting silently into secret fear. We keep moving forward with determination, but the steps that were just skipping with joy have fallen into a more regular rhythm.

To fill the silence we try to sing the songs we have known in our bondage, but they seem odd and out of place now. We rehearse the stories of our captors' defeat as we marched out of captivity but soon run out of new words. Periodically we grab another's hand or arm and shake it vigorously in celebration, but mostly we are quiet, lost in our thoughts of freedom but also in the questions of what exactly that might mean.

Following the Covid pandemic of the early 2020s, many local churches joined the plethora of retail businesses advertising on social media. Shiny, modern ads were posted in hopes of drawing young believers back to the old wineskins of worship. Some of us remember the images—hands and arms raised, faces contorted, lights and cameras placed just right, reminding us of former itera-tions. Other times and places in the past where we promoted the new-and-improved version of church marked by significant nu-merical success, an era later termed *mega*.

Somewhere along the way, our worship gathering places got re-packaged to look like popular concert venues, complete with wide lobbies, coffee bars, and gift shops. But now huge sanctuaries with seating for thousands, big screens, stage lighting, and booming

sound systems were sitting half-empty and out of use as our invest-
ments in place resulted in the neglect and exclusion of people.

Then life screeched to a halt. The lights went out. The doors were
shuttered and we were left to sit for days, weeks, months, a year reflecting on what had been. Reflection led to anger and anger to
outrage, and the slow exodus began away from this modern re-
packaged brand of "church"—an institution that, whether through
ignorance, silence, or active participation, was found to be complicit
in a myriad of societal ills. Angry voices flooded the digital airways,
and things once held sacred became targets of public criticism and
ridicule. Many watched in satisfaction or sadness as the churches
that birthed and nurtured them imploded in a heap of bricks and
mortar dust or slipped into silent irrelevance.

Eventually the loud voices became whispers and the social demo-
lition crews, leaving us with far less, rolled away. We were left to
march through the pain and rubble on our own. Today, in this space
between what was and what shall be, we are again reflecting on what
exactly we believe. Pondering a Jesus turned from blond to brown.
Attempting to piece together a faith that's big enough to hold us in
our difference and disagreements. Longing to access a love that is
supernatural, reaching across racial constructs and ethnic identities,
political parties and various doctrinal and cultural practices and
points of view.

The question is, as children of the instant and the immediate, do
we have the patience to wait for it? Can we summon the faith to
believe? Can we press through the tension pulling us back toward
the destructive familiar and lean instead toward a promised hope
not yet seen? Time will tell.

For now, we walk through the dust on our way to better, salvaging what remains useful of our former conviction. Faith, hope, love, grace, salvation, and truth are gathered and carried in tired arms toward the next. While we are creating, we are remembering. Grabbing reliable pieces from what was to fashion something new. We are exhilarated and terrified. Resolute in our convictions while quietly grieving that which is lost. Someone picks up a pen and begins to write a new song. Another once again rehearses the old story. And we walk and we wait and we write and we pray and we work and we sing as we look toward the promise and press on.

> Listen carefully, I am about to do a new thing,
> Now it will spring forth;
> Will you not be aware of it?
> I will even put a road in the wilderness,
> Rivers in the desert. (Isaiah 43:19)

24

SOMETIMES THE WILDERNESS CALLS FOR AN UNFAIR FIGHT

SOMETIMES GOD PLACES US or allows us into situations where we appear greatly disadvantaged in order to demonstrate his supreme power and divine love. We see this play out again and again throughout Scripture and quite often in our daily lives as well. It's not comfortable. Sometimes it's downright painful. But in this place of extreme need and divine dependence, we experience profound grace and a welcome intimacy with the living God.

For sixteen years, with little to no budget, two amazingly talented volunteers and I ran an eight-week summer youth development program for fifty-plus kids. There were many times in the middle of it where I felt like Gideon with his small band of warriors up against an army of thousands. Every year began as an impossible task to secure academic instruction, artistic enrichment, leadership development, team building, and recreational activity along with meals, transportation, and supplies. Yet every year we had the opportunity to watch God show up, provide everything we needed, and impact lives.

It never made sense on paper, doing so much with so little, and yet that is often God's way. Tiny mustard seeds, fish scraps and bread crumbs, David versus Goliath, and Gideon's three hundred. Harriet's railroad, Sojourner's truth, Fannie's courage, and Martin's dream. God is always using the small, the poor, and the least to bring down the mighty. We win not because we have superior strategies. We win not because we are smarter. Not because we are inherently stronger or possess better tools or weapons. We win simply because God has decided to give us the victory.

> Then the LORD said to Gideon, "There are too many people with you for Me to hand over Midian to them, otherwise Israel will boast [about themselves] against Me, saying, 'My own power has rescued me.'" (Judges 7:2)

God repeatedly made Gideon reduce the size of his army, from thirty-two thousand to ten thousand to three hundred. This seems extreme, but the reality is that since the victory was assured, Gideon could have gone against Midian with ten. When God decides to hand something over to us, to give us a victory, he has the means, the plan, and the power to do so. One of our few meaningful contributions is obedience. However, our obedience is often in proportion to our faith.

Sometimes, like Gideon, despite God's sure word, I struggle to believe. I too want to put out a fleece, ask a neighbor, phone a friend, and get twelve confirmations. We doubt because we think victory depends not on God but on us. God said to Moses in Exodus 3:7, "I have in fact seen the affliction (suffering, desolation) of My people who are in Egypt, and have heard their cry because of their task-masters (oppressors); for I know their pain and suffering." Despite this clear statement of God's intention to deliver his own people,

Moses proceeds to give a list of reasons why God's plan is not going to work based on Moses' own abilities or the lack thereof.

"I am not important enough to talk to Pharoah."

"They will ask who sent me (by whose authority am I come)."

"They won't believe me."

"I don't speak well enough. I have a speech problem."

To which God responded, "Who has made man's mouth? . . . Is it not I, the Lord? Now then go, and I, even I, will be with your mouth." (Exodus 4:11-12).

Yet even this is not enough for Moses. His reply, basically, is, "I think you should send someone else."

Are we like Moses, coming up with our laundry list of reasons we cannot do what God has clearly said he will do with, in, or through us? Are we deceived into thinking that victory depends on our efforts or abilities? Are we like Gideon, dismissing God's direct promises and not finding comfort or assurance until we hear them through the mouth of a man? Or can we, by faith, believe that God is all he says he is and can do all he purposes to do based on his own sufficiency, sovereignty, and power? He chooses us, but as Jesus said, "From these stones God is able to raise up children (descendants) for Abraham" (Matthew 3:9).

The wilderness is a desert, a land of mirage. Things are often not as they appear. We cannot walk by sight or lean on our own understanding. We must take our three hundred or thirty or three and by faithful obedience march to the place he sends us. Sometimes we are armed only with our trumpets of praise and our empty pitchers of hope, but we trust that, for this battle and those that lie ahead, they will be enough.

25

TRUSTING GOD IS A DECISION

TRUSTING GOD IS A DECISION. It is a choice we make every day, a step we take over the side and out of the boat. It is not based on weather conditions or the size of the waves but rather our faith in the Master. For me, water walking began long before I approached the side of the boat. That kind of faith begins as a tiny seed when we get our first real glimpse of Christ.

The church of my childhood was a large church for the time, probably a little over a thousand "on roll." Likely about six or seven hundred on an average Sunday morning, a hundred to a hundred and fifty children and youth alone. On Friday nights, in a small section of a side room in the basement, about ten of us late teens and young adults would gather for a rogue Bible study. It was nothing like the elaborate youth wings of the suburban churches I would later visit in the South as an adult, with their colorful furnishings, shelves of hardback books, thick rugs, bean bags, and comfy couches. No, it was the kind of room with brown panel accordion curtains that served as movable walls and a block tile floor that formed a checkered pattern. A space with fluorescent lights, cold metal folding chairs, and maybe a metal desk or small wood podium in the front.

The leader of the study wasn't the deacon or the youth pastor or even the Sunday school leader you'd expect. Instead he was a trustee, one of the money guys—a role often reserved for college-educated folks in the congregation. For some reason, in his free time at the end of a long day at the end of a long week, he chose to spend his time with us to teach us about the kingdom of God.

Greg talked about the kingdom as if it was Narnia—a world we were intrinsically a part of though we mostly couldn't see it. He taught us about its customs and people. He challenged us to learn its language and govern ourselves by its laws—the laws of grace and love and truth. Most importantly he told us about its King and our own roles in the kingdom and the profound responsibility we had to fulfill them. He pushed us to think about and apply the Scriptures to our daily lives and the world around us and helped us believe that with the power of God we were capable of infiltrating its systems and taking them over.

In time, through new eyes, we began to see the kingdom in the marvelous and majestic but also in the ordinary and mundane. The kingdom was all around us and, like Neo, we began to believe. I got a glimpse of the resurrected Christ and wanted more and more.

Soon the day came when I could see him walking on the water. Though my natural mind struggled with that reality, the spirit agreed. Before I knew it, like Peter, I found myself shouting, "Lord, if it is really you, command me to come to you on the water."

And immediately I heard the invitation, "Come!"

Jesus is not afraid or wavering. He invites us into this confidence, this rest that comes with trust. "Come," he says.

Step out of your small boat of safety. Climb over your railings of false security. Step out of the fragile vessel of your fear onto the deep, wide ocean of God's grace. Then start walking with steady, sure feet toward the Master of your sea of doubts, the captain of your fretful soul, and believe. Believe he is able to keep you from falling. Believe he is more than enough. Believe that the waves that threaten and mock you are subject to his word and you will never be beyond his reach.

I walked to the side and climbed over the rail. I entered the wardrobe. I chose the red pill. I looked down at the watery darkness, extended my trembling leg, and felt my hand let go. Trust is a decision, a choice we make every day. If we wait for the sky to clear or the waves to calm or our hearts to stop pounding, we will never move but remain, heart longing, feet firm on the ground. Our trust is not in our abilities or in the details of a meticulous well-thought-out plan. Our faith is in the awesome power of our big, amazing God and our confidence in his simple invitation: to come.

26

BY HELL OR WHITEWATER

S OME YEARS AGO I WAS STARTING a job that required a team-building retreat. This "retreat" included tent camping, sleeping on the floor of a church, and whitewater rafting. Now, anyone who knows me knows this was all way outside of my comfort zone. I almost changed my mind about accepting the position. Really. For those of us who have spent our entire lives getting to some comfort, we don't see "roughing it" as any kind of fun. But since I love Jesus and believed this job was somehow in his plan, I decided to accept the job and the "retreat" that came with it.

Now while sleeping on the floor or in a tent in the woods is its own type of hell, the prospect of whitewater rafting produced the most dread in my mind. Whitewater by definition screams *DANGER*. Whitewater is formed when the slope of a river increases enough to disturb its normally smooth flow and create turbulence, a bubbly and rolling current, which makes the frothy water appear white. Think of airplane turbulence and how much you love that. Now think of that in the water. Exactly.

I am a black girl from West Philly. The river is something we drive by on our way to work. Yes, we have Boat House Row with its many rowing clubs along the Schuylkill River, but growing up, not one of the people in those long, skinny boats looked like me. We didn't have a crew team at my high school. We didn't have rafts either, and I was good with that. But I said yes because I love Jesus.

> I will instruct you and teach you in the way you should go;
> I will counsel you [who are willing to learn] with My eye
>> upon you. (Psalm 32:8)

Rafting in whitewater is really an exercise in obedience. No previous experience is required. With the proper equipment and a knowledgeable guide, almost anyone can do it. Also, it isn't something you do alone (that would be kayaking, another irrational activity). The idea is to work together as a team to accomplish the goal of navigating the rapids to reach the destination.

Prior to getting in the raft the team members receive equipment—a helmet, a life vest, and a paddle. Beyond that you have only your team and the sound of your guide's voice. Training for this life-or-death adventure (my description) comes down to learning to follow a few basic commands—paddle forward, paddle backward, left back, right back, high side, stop, and lean in. The guide explains what each command means and the proper way to do it. Following the commands individually is not enough to ensure a successful journey. It is also important to work together as a team. Matching the depth and pace of each paddle stroke, the starts and the stops, should get everyone down the river safely. It is also vital to know your position in the raft. The commands have little meaning if you don't know right from left, forward from back, or where center is. Finally, you must trust your guide and his knowledge of the river, its turns, its drops, its current, and the obstacles ahead that are unseen by you.

> Surely when the great waters [of trial and distressing times]
>   overflow they will not reach [the spirit in] him.
> You are my hiding place; You, LORD, protect me from trouble;
> You surround me with songs and shouts of deliverance.
>   (Psalm 32:6-7)

The past few weeks, months, and even years have been filled with the turbulence of whitewater, leaving many of us feeling shaken by the unexpected bumps of hatred or disoriented by the crashing waves of illness or grief. We've been paddling so long our arms are sore and exhaustion is beginning to set in.

Rest assured that the godly have a hiding place in times of trouble. Even when the turbulence of life is rising up and crashing against us, God surrounds us with songs of praise. When we are disoriented, we must remember our training. Remember our position in the raft. And when avoiding impact is impossible, we must lean in to our center and hold on.

> I will instruct you and teach you in the way you should go.
> I will counsel you [who are willing to learn] with My eye
>   upon you. (Psalm 32:8)

Even while we are going, God is teaching us the way and what we need to do to get there. We may not always be able to see the way forward, but we don't need to be afraid. God will guide us with his eye. The Lord sees the path ahead because the all-knowing, omnipresent God is already there. Remember you are not alone. If you panic and start moving at your own pace, going your own way, you put yourself and everyone else in the raft in danger.

Conditions right now may feel scary or appear hopeless, but that is when we must listen for his commands. Paddle back. Paddle forward. Stop and lean in.

29

FOUND IN THE WILD

ALWAYS PICTURED THE WILDERNESS AS WILD, dry, and barren, because that's how I'd heard people talk about it. I think of crumbly sand and prickly cactus and brown, leafless trees. I think of extreme temperatures and air so thick with heat you can barely breathe in. I think of the desert and dying, the dry bones of unfortunate animals picked clean.

With these images in my mind, the wilderness seems like a place to avoid. A harsh training ground for would-be soldiers at best. But there is more to the wilderness than I originally imagined. More images to consider and receive.

> But he himself traveled a day's journey into the wilderness, and he came and sat down under a juniper tree and asked [God] that he might die. (1 Kings 19:4)

Not long ago, my husband and I and a few friends made our way to Joshua Tree, an interesting national park about 130 miles east of Los Angeles. This park is located in the Mojave Desert, and it features desert landscapes, rock formations, and countless odd, some might even say ugly, trees called Joshua trees, which give the park its name. Besides the paved road that runs through the middle of the park, there are no neat paths or trails. No plethora of colorful signs or placards. No tree-shaded campsites or shiny, tiled bathrooms.

Instead, its beauty is in the time-worn clefts of the rocks, the cool darkness of its caves, the contrast of tan rock beside vibrant green, wild shrubs beneath cobalt blue sky. Most notably, there is a surprising attraction of the eye to the misshapen succulents that dot the rocky landscape. The trees whose thick, shaggy-topped, goalpost arms challenge previously held ideas of beauty, encourage us to reconsider if not embrace outright.

Yes, the wilderness can be wild and uncultivated, but perhaps that does not speak of death as much as freedom. The wilderness is uncontrolled with room to be changed and reimagined. Perhaps rather than a place of death, the wilderness is a space for transformation. A place where we remember all that we were and discover (again?) all that we might become. Yes, we are emptied and even petrified in this wasteland, but it's only so we can be broken open and poured out in new form for greater purpose and service.

After all, wilderness may not be a barren, uninhabited tract of land but an uncultivated garden where plants grow wild. Truth be told, there is something within me that longs for that freedom where we can move and change and become. It is often in that space that we encounter the holy and rediscover who we were born and are reborn to be.

Throughout Scripture, God shows up in the desert and in the garden and on the mountain to meet and commune and confront. To connect.

> There he came to a cave and spent the night in it; and behold, the word of the Lord came to him, and He said to him, "What are you doing here, Elijah?" (1 Kings 19:9)

Some of us have fallen away from him while sitting in the middle of a cushioned, temperature-controlled church sanctuary. Others have lost themselves in the thick of daily battles or under the soul-numbing routines of a safe, well-ordered life. But here amid the dusty terrain of our wilderness, without the familiar laid-out paths and well-lit signs for what comes next, we are left with a much-needed disorientation. It shakes us from our stupors and interrupts our daydreaming. It causes us to reconsider the things we've over-looked or dismissed as ugly or unimportant. It causes us to think and to feel and to reengage all our senses and to hear again, like the first time, the voice of God.

We were hesitant, not knowing what to expect when we began our visit to Joshua Tree. Our slow ride through the park took hours, beginning at dusk and into the evening of one day and continuing morning through afternoon of the next. Over the course of our journey, resistance turned to embrace. We did not change the park. But our willingness to listen to its silence, to consider the lines and texture of its landscape and to stare at the shocking magnificence of its nighttime sky, changed us. It expanded our view of its Creator.

We are not in control in this wilderness. We are small and vulnerable and exposed. And it is reasonable, at times, to feel afraid. This vulnerability opens us to our need for the living God. Despite our resistance and trepidation, we can enter the wilderness sure of one thing only—that as we make our way through its tangled expanse, he will be there.

28

THIS MIDNIGHT

O **VER THE PAST FEW MONTHS** I've realized how weary I've become. Shooting after shooting, tragedy upon tragedy, death, grief, and more death. Should we draft another statement? Can I write another post? Find another level of outrage or cry another tear? I feel all I am capable of is a deeply drawn breath followed by a long, slow sigh. This is weariness.

I know we are not where we were. I see the subtle changes and sense the incremental progress of the past several years. But the light of hope is struggling under the relentless attack of darkness.

Where do we go for relief when our celebrations are interrupted by gunfire? Who will protect us when the faces that pursue, abuse, and take our lives look much like our own? Do we have the energy to endure after another election cycle? Do we even want to try?

In the darkest darkness before the coming dawn, at the edge of promised victory, we hang by a hopeful thread, waiting, sure of only one thing—he who promised is faithful.

I will lift up my eyes to the hills [of Jerusalem]—
From where shall my help come?

My help comes from the LORD,
Who made heaven and earth.

He will not allow your foot to slip;
He who keeps you will not slumber.

Behold, He who keeps Israel
Will neither slumber [briefly] nor sleep [soundly].

The LORD is your keeper;
The LORD is your shade on your right hand.

The sun will not strike you by day,
Nor the moon by night.

The LORD will protect you from all evil;
He will keep your life.

The LORD will guard your going out and your coming in
        [everything that you do]
From this time forth and forever. (Psalm 121)

When we have nothing left but God, we have enough.
    We have love.
    We have the way.
    We have the truth.
    We have the life.
    We have justice.

When we cannot find it by sight, we will trust it by faith.

When we are too weary to go on, we will take the cue from our bodies and wait.

When we wait, we will receive new strength

to mount up and soar

to run and not grow weary

to walk and not faint

There is rest for the weary. I will find it knowing that even this present darkness, this midnight, must submit to him.

29

THE WILDERNESS IS NOT SAFE

T HE PATH TO FREEDOM IS NOT SAFE. Who has ever made their way from bondage to freedom without risk? There are always things to go under, around, or through. Barriers and obstacles, one after another, designed to limit progress and make escape seem futile.

I met God in the wilderness of the unfamiliar. The kind of place where you can see only one step in front of you and have to call on Jesus to take that. Where the math doesn't add up and the map has no coordinates and all the strategy has gone out of the plan. In these spaces God shows up as a knowing in your gut or a whisper in your ear asking, *Do you trust me?* Sometimes it's a call to cross a state or the country or the ocean to learn from serving a people you do not know. Sometimes it's a weight on your heart when you've started out the door that compels you to stay instead.

The problem is, "safety" sells. Marketing execs have built billion-dollar industries convincing us of the perils lying in wait for us at every step outside our comfort zones. We are encouraged to play it safe. Don't venture too far. Don't stir up trouble. Don't ask too many questions. Just go along. Trouble is, the one we follow does not espouse to this. Repeatedly the people of God are called to be courageous and fearless. To step into the unknown and the disruptive.

> Have I not commanded you? Be strong and courageous! Do not be terrified or dismayed (intimidated), for the LORD your God is with you wherever you go. (Joshua 1:9)

We are warned by humanity to "Be careful!" while we hear God saying, "Be courageous." There is no promise or implication of safety in the Bible. Time after time we see ordinary people making risk-filled choices that lead them not into destruction but into extraordinary life.

Mordecai calls Esther out from the safety of silence to a potentially life-threatening confrontation with the king in order to stop the genocide of her people. Gideon is led by God to confront the Midian army of thousands with just three hundred men. Jesus calls his disciples from the routines and trades of their day-to-day existence to the angry mobs and stormy seas of new life. Throughout history, men and women have chosen to walk away from the safety of the majority and the comfortable into the wilderness of the unknown and the uncertain. Because on the other side of that desert is liberty.

I've often wondered, if Moses was able to get from Egypt to Midian to Mount Horeb and back to Egypt without crossing the Red Sea, why did God lead the Israelites to pass through it? Perhaps there was another way to get to where they were going, but this was the path that stopped their enemies' pursuit. The story of the journey through the waves and the wilderness would become the reference point to undergird the Jewish faith even to this present day. It was that experience that distinguished them as the chosen people and brought fear to the hearts of their enemies. It was the beginning of their transition from slaves to sons and marked God, not Pharoah, as the only sovereign Lord in their lives.

Like Israel, many of us have cried out to God for freedom. We want to see change in our personal lives or communities. We long to be delivered from a nationalist faith and a colonized church. We want the world to be changed, less violent, more just, but what are we willing to give up to get there? What are we willing to do? Where are we willing to go? The Spirit of God is urging us forward toward the new and the next that we have cried out for God to give us. Yet we find ourselves clinging to the familiarity of Egypt or looking for an alternate route. God may be leading us in a direction that appears more challenging and dangerous, but perhaps it is the course we must take for our transition from bondage to freedom. Unfortunately, we too often choose a vague, small life and a feeble, small faith that is safe.

As early as kindergarten we are taught it is best to just be quiet. We learn to follow the feet of the one ahead of us. To walk in step and stay single file. To operate within the boundaries of the schoolyard. We play the games that are taught to us and pledge allegiance to the flag. And almost always we walk and color within the lines. But Jesus is still whispering to the called-out ones, calling us out into the deep and into the wild. Because while the journey of faith and freedom may involve many things yet unimagined, one thing is certain. It will not be safe.

He who loves father or mother more than Me is not worthy of Me; and he who loves son or daughter more than Me is not worthy of Me. And he who does not take his cross [expressing a willingness to endure whatever may come] and follow Me [believing in Me, conforming to My example in living and, if need be, suffering or perhaps dying because of faith in Me] is not worthy of Me. Whoever finds his life [in this world] will [eventually] lose it [through death], and whoever loses his life [in this world] for My sake will find it [that is, life with Me for all eternity]. (Matthew 10:37-39)

30

BY ANOTHER NAME

After a little while the bystanders came up and said

to Peter, "Surely you are one of them too."

MATTHEW 26:73

IN THE DAYS FOLLOWING the 2016 and 2024 elections, many people were caught in shock and disbelief. As much as we wanted to deny it, the numbers didn't lie. The majority of the self-identified white evangelical church had voted for American exceptionalism, for us vs. them, for "no we won't" instead of "yes we can." And amid the chaos that followed, many began to back away from the body formerly known as the church. When the Covid pandemic closed the physical doors in 2020, it was easy for some to shift to drinking their Sunday morning coffees on the sofa in pajamas and to remain there long after the doors had opened again.

Listening to people talk about the church is like having a conversation with someone referring to themselves in the third person. We talk about needing change as though it were something that had to occur in others and about the church as though we were not part of its skin and bones. But this time between Egypt and Canaan is as much about God preparing us for the new church as it is about preparing a new church for us. This time in the wilderness has been painfully revealing, and over the course of the journey we have been exposed. In the rough terrain of our country's social conflict, the spiritual wig and high heels have been forsaken. In the heat of the conflict, our made-up faces have begun to drip and run. Our God is not interested in our carefully coifed outward appearances, tightly timed worship services, big names, fancy edifices, or meticulous run-of-show.

It is not just church structure that is being made over. It is we his people who are being made new. We have always been the worship, sermons, and edifice of his building. We therefore are the thing he is making again. We are the wine and the new wineskins. In the heat of this fermentation process, it is God's people who must be transformed. The church is not something separate from or outside of us. It will not be rebuilt with creative new programs or rebranding but on a return to our heart's confession of Jesus as the Christ. His way as the only way. His word as truth. His blood as the only hope for abundant life.

I found church in the open arms of his people. It was in the faithful presence and walk of a shepherding pastor and in the lessons of choir directors and teachers who welcomed me into their homes. The Bible was taught by example over chicken and potato salad at the annual picnic and in the loving correction that might happen on the long car ride home. The church wasn't so much the place we went as the experience we shared together. After a particularly powerful message and a moving worship, someone would often remark, "Didn't we have church?" and another would reply, "Girl, we had church today!" This meant we had connected with God and one another in a way that was seen and felt by all.

If the church has dissolved into mere routine or institution or, worse, a political weapon of the majority to oppress the few, it has happened either with our consent or as a result of our passivity. In any case, it does not happen without you and me. Unfortunately, we sometimes stand silent like Peter, warming himself by the fire while Jesus is being interrogated nearby. And when the accusations come, we try to separate ourselves as the exception, not realizing how our speech gives us away.

We cannot dismember the Lord's body and expect it be healthy. We cannot dismember ourselves from it and expect to be whole living as an amputated limb. As I seek God in prayer for myself and others and press into the grace available to me, I bring spiritual health to myself and the body, his church, which Christ has ordained to bring the fruit of love, joy, peace, patience, goodness, gentleness, meekness, and faith to a hurting world.

"Surely you are one of them too . . . " (Matthew 26:73)

Jesus did not choose an individual to represent him here on earth but rather a people. How we come together and live together both in love and correction, in righteousness and lament, is how we make Christ visible to the world. The discomfort we may feel in the process is God pressing out the new wine for his wineskins. The doors of our broken institutions are closed and closing, but the arms of God's church are open and even the gates of hell shall not overpower it.

Part Four

FINDING
OURSELVES

31

COSTUMES AND COSPLAY

Therefore if anyone is in Christ [that is, grafted in, joined to Him
by faith in Him as Savior], he is a new creature [reborn and
renewed by the Holy Spirit]; the old things [the previous moral
and spiritual condition] have passed away. Behold, new things
have come [because spiritual awakening brings a new life].

2 CORINTHIANS 5:17

'VE NEVER BEEN A BIG FAN OF HALLOWEEN, but I've noticed it becoming more and more an adult celebration over the past decade
or two. People love taking a night off from the normalcy of their
regular lives to dress up and become someone or something else. In
similar fashion, cosplay—a subculture of costume roleplaying, a
$4.8 billion industry (at the time of publication)—is projected to
grow to an $8.7 billion industry by 2033. New fans press into the
fantasy pretending through costume and makeup to be their favorite
movie and anime characters. There are festivals and events with
thousands of people in attendance from dozens of countries. While

Halloween may last for a night or a weekend, numerous cosplay events are held throughout the year.

While cosplay is popular and putting on costumes is fun, this is not what it means to be in Christ. Our Christian identity is not something we put on for an event or Sunday worship occasion and later remove like makeup that we wash down the drain of our daily lives. We are rather being transplanted into the bone and marrow of the living Christ. Slowly, day by day, we are becoming one with him. Fusing, like the engrafted branch we are, into the divine vine for the purpose of bearing fruit.

Throughout this life we shed skin, shed hair, shed clothes. Stepping out of the old and into something new. As we walk through the wilderness periods of life, the challenge of the trek forces us to lighten our load, to let go of the things that do not matter. We re-evaluate our priorities and redefine our needs. We shed. And then, stripped of our former outward wrappings, we can begin to reimagine ourselves.

The Scriptures speak frequently about putting off and putting on, laying aside and taking up various things. In Ephesians, Paul writes to the believers:

> Regarding your previous way of life, you put off your old self [completely discard your former nature] . . . and be continually renewed in the spirit of your mind [having a fresh, untarnished mental and spiritual attitude], and put on the new self [the regenerated and renewed nature], created in God's image, [godlike] in the righteousness and holiness of the truth. (Ephesians 4:22-24)

I've found the taking off part to be comparably easier and may even provide some much-needed relief. But putting on the new seems significantly more difficult. We are creatures of habit, resistant to change. Isaiah describes salvation as a garment as though putting on righteousness were as simple as slipping on a bathrobe. Perhaps, but only if that bathrobe is a couple sizes too big with weights in the pockets and flapping in the gale force winds of fleshly resistance. No. Putting on this newness of life is neither simple nor easy, but perhaps because it must be preceded by stepping in.

What does it mean to be in Christ, "in him"? I think often about him being in me but less frequently about me being in him, being in God. What does that even mean?

In Christ, I am triumphant.

In Christ, I have victory.

In Christ, I am a new creation.

But what does it mean to be in him? When we get dressed, we say we are in our clothes. Our clothes become an outward expression of our identity and help reveal us to the world. When we accept God's gift of salvation we are baptized, immersed into Christ, dying to our old selves and resurrecting in our new identity, our Christ skin. In my Christ identity, the old natural, fleshly me can begin to recess and fall away. I begin to see through my new Christ eyes, hear the voice of others through my new Christ ears. Christlike empathy can replace my calloused heart and divine humility my closed mind.

In Christ, time loses its preeminence so the constant rush and hustle that tends to keep me from reflection can grow quiet and wonder can reemerge. In Christ there is no room for fear. Faith and peace fill up that space. Rest is now guilt-free and deserved. In Christ I am made new.

Dress-up is fun for a season. Cosplay can be enjoyed for a while. But plastic swords are no match for the real dangers of the wild and stage makeup runs in the heat and sweat of suffering. Hidden in him, though, grafted in and held by his grace, I can live and continue to grow even when life is hard.

Then, and only then, can I begin to take up and put on the spiritual clothes, the character and lifestyle, that identify me as his.

The name of the LORD is a strong tower;
The righteous runs to it and is safe. (Proverbs 18:10)

32

LEARNING TO SING IN A STRANGE LAND

PERIODICALLY, AS AN INDIVIDUAL OR A CHURCH, we are led away from the familiar and into the challenge that is wilderness. Here the trees are sparse and the path less defined. We get disoriented and confused and reacquainted with thirst. When our legs grow weary and our bellies growl, we remember and seek the one our soul desires.

While the wilderness is a place of remembrance, it is also a place of discovery and preparation. It was in the wilderness years that my knowledge of God moved from my head to my heart. From theory to experience, from principle to practice. Stripped down in the wilderness, I discovered what I truly believed and became more fully aware of the depth, and sometimes shallowness, of my faith. Over time I grew stronger and more certain of God's presence and power. Again and again the truth of God's Word was tested, and I learned that I could indeed step out on it. I put my weight on it, timidly at first, and then, out of necessity, with full force. It held me. He held me.

In the wilderness my family met the challenge of raising support, a construct of white evangelical ministry that financially favors the well-off or well-connected. We were neither. So I leaned into the truth that God is Jehovah Jireh and watched him provide food and clothing for me and my family. I poured out to the children and relatives of my new community from the overflow of what he was daily pouring into me. I met God in the quiet stillness of the early morning hours, often on my knees with a face full of tears. He met me as El-Shaddai, the All Sufficient One, the God who is more than enough.

One particularly cold winter an ice storm hit Atlanta and we were without power for four days. After the first two days we talked about perhaps borrowing money from family to head to a hotel, but by then we were aware that ours was one of the few houses in our neighborhood with a gas stove. With schools closed, our small home became the place where the neighborhood children hung out, warmed by the four burners we kept at full blast, along with an open oven door, throughout the day. The heat from our tiny kitchen spilled into the dining and living rooms. We played games and laughed and ate, sharing meals and stories, finding Immanuel in the evening's candlelight and in the presence of one another.

While we showed up to worship on Sundays at the large Baptist church less than a mile from our house in those early years, my hours there began to pale in comparison to the way I was coming to know Jesus during the week. In the midst of all that southern hospitality and sweet tea charm, I often felt isolated and alone. I felt like Dorothy in Oz. I missed the friendships and culture of my northern city and, for the first time in my life, I was far away from the place I knew as home. But obedience had brought me to this strange land,

and within its dry and lonely landscape family was redefined, as were many things I thought I'd previously known.

I started to see God on the prayer walks we began taking one Sunday a month around our community and in the smiles of the elderly neighbors who frequented our home for dinner on Wednesday nights. I began to hear him in the laughter of my children as my husband told silly stories before putting them to bed and through my failed attempts at gardening as he talked to me about planting seeds in the hard heart of red Georgia clay. I sang to him outside the confines of the church choir loft and he sang to me new songs in melodies not previously learned and through genres formerly unknown.

I became a preacher within the walls of my northern Baptist church, but I began to preach in the boundless freedom of the wilderness. I was educated in the lecture halls of the northern university but I became an educator in the southern streets of the wilderness.

We may learn of and come to know God in us in the comfort and safety of the church building. But we often come to find ourselves in God through the struggles of the wilderness.

> Consider it nothing but joy, my brothers and sisters, whenever you fall into various trials. Be assured that the testing of your faith [through experience] produces endurance [leading to spiritual maturity, and inner peace]. And let endurance have its perfect result and do a thorough work, so that you may be perfect and completely developed [in your faith], lacking in nothing. (James 1:2-4)

33

A FAMILIAR FEAST

NOT TOO LONG AGO, I had the opportunity to travel to my hometown of Philadelphia to attend a benefit concert in honor of a musician I've known and respected for many years. I was excited, because not only was I going to hear the music that had sustained me through the early years of my adulthood, I was also going to share the experience with two of my closest childhood friends who would also be there.

The girls and I connected before the event over a meal at a popular spot known for its soul food menu that was close to my old neighborhood. We talked nonstop, looked at old pictures, and snapped a few new ones. After lunch we made our way through familiar sections of town made new through gentrification or obsolete through neglect. When we finally arrived on the north side of the city at the large black Baptist church, we joined the stream of faces filing into the sanctuary.

When the music started, I settled back against the pew and closed my eyes. Feeling the familiar curve of the smooth wood beneath me and the vibration of the Hammond organ swelling all around, I felt the tension leaving my body. As the afternoon went on, we sang along with the old songs we remembered and clapped and swayed with the new. Before long hands were lifted, tears were falling, and my lips were moving silently with words of praise.

Sitting in the back of that church I realized how hungry I had been, how starved for the familiar rhythms, the call and response, the cadence and flavor of the worship experience of my youth. I had spent the last two and a half decades in white, multicultural, or online church spaces living off justice talks and what sometimes felt like crumbs of the Spirit. I was hungry, starving for more.

Historically, there has always been a union between the black church in America and justice. Civic engagement was not a distraction from the gospel or a social add-on. It was faith lived out in the streets. Or, as Dr. Cornel West puts it, "Justice is what love looks like in public." We did not have to choose between our spiritual lives and our physical well-being. Indeed, while it was far from perfect, the black church was the one place where we could acknowledge and care for our whole selves without apology. But somewhere along the line we began to be complacent, and a more educated and affluent black middle class began to distance itself from the community's pain. In some cases, a desire for legitimacy in the white gaze began to separate us from each other.

Young people took to the streets in 2020 with desperate determination to be heard by a failing government. Older folks, disillusioned by what appeared to be an out-of-touch or disinterested church, joined them. They marched and they shouted. They cried and they chanted. They formed a new kind of congregation, creating pulpits on the hoods of parked cars and turning protest songs into hymns of comfort and solidarity.

Others were discipled in the homes of the growing movement and got inspired by the fiery text they found online. We met or were reintroduced to a liberation gospel and with excitement entered the baptismal waters of the just. And as the chorus swelled to a fever pitch around the globe, we began to imagine that we could see the horizon of our long-awaited jubilee. We raised our fists and hugged our friends, and we glanced over our shoulders at the sight of a waning church now falling out of view.

For a time we fed sufficiently from that justice church banquet, sustained by the delicious sugar rush of hope. But over time the crowds thinned, quieted, and then disappeared, and the songs of the street now seem distant, hard to recall, and far away. The progress made, though undeniable, is still not what we had hoped for, and evil, though temporarily shaken, has regrouped. We found ourselves in the midst of many battles. We learned to exist and move without apology. Now, neck deep in the latest waves of injustice, some of us have also found ourselves spiritually hungry and moving alone.

From its inception, the church has been hampered by the imperfections of her people. Yet she has also been made mighty by our union. Or more precisely, by our communion. There is power in the simple meal served at the table in the house of God. Sitting shoulder to shoulder with other sojourners, sharing bread. Likely because we are an organism, sometimes buried under the weight of institution, but nonetheless conceived and birthed by Almighty God.

Yes, it's been contaminated over time by the poisonous plants of greed and pride or tainted by misguided attempts at quick, unsustainable growth. But the church still holds the soul food our hearts remember and, in the hunger of the present time, she calls us home. Back to a table that's familiar yet, by the power of God, made new.

I hugged my friends goodbye as the music ended. I breathed deeply and made my way out of the sanctuary, through the doors, and to the car. Dr. King said, "The arc of the moral universe is long, but it bends toward justice."[1] Glad to be reminded that I don't have to make that long trek out in the world alone.

34

SABBATH

WAS READING A FAMILIAR PASSAGE in the book of beginnings when I came across these words:

And by the seventh day God completed His work which He had done, and He rested (ceased) on the seventh day from all His work which he had done. (Genesis 2:2)

I am sure I've read those words many times before, but for the first time I wondered why God needed or wanted to rest. Does God get tired? That didn't seem to make sense, seeing that God, unlike us, is not limited by a physical body in need of sleep. And God didn't lay bricks or prepare reports or sit through long meetings while forming the earth and heavens. Was speaking the world into existence extremely tiring? So much so that he set aside an entire day to rest from the exertion?

Creation is the work of imagination and ingenuity and hope and faith. It is an effort of the mind and spirit. The body simply executes what the mind and spirit create. God is the original artist, designer, and architect. He looked on nothing, imagined something, and made it so. Light and shadow, line and form, color and texture birthed in his every word. From the simple amoeba to the amazing lifegiving womb, concept became creature in perfection until he stepped back in satisfaction and called it good.

And then he rested, not out of fatigue or necessity but rather deliberate, intentional choice. He rested from creating to enjoy what was created. The Sabbath is not about the body, as God did not have one. Rest is for the mind and spirit, an invitation to enjoy creation and the presence of Creator and one another. We are invited each week into a rest from labor as God rested from all of his work.

Thinking on this prompted another question: What is work? Work is the effort to produce or accomplish something, the daily grind, the race for the rat. For many of us it is not the pleasure or satisfaction of creation but task upon task, repetitive motion, pushing out the product, crossing off the list. It is what feels like endless effort for little reward for the basic privilege of merely surviving. For many of us our work is not creative and rest is not restorative. Our rest is simply a pause to prepare for more work. It is not sabbath.

Sabbath is an invitation to step back at the end of a week of labor to reflect on what we have done. More than an invitation, it is a command, a day set apart from the others for God. It is the Lord's sabbath and permission to enjoy the fruit of that labor.

At rest we don't need to produce or achieve anything. We can do simply for the pleasure of doing. Or we can be still and cease from doing for the pleasure that comes from stillness. Sometimes in that pleasurable pause we rediscover beauty and wonder. We meet up with relatives and friends for laughter and long cups of coffee. We sink into soothing hot water and mounds of scented bubbles and let the stress of the week melt away. Clenched muscles relax. Shallow breathing becomes deep and slow and the trauma of that encounter, that conversation, that hateful experience begins to fade.

The beauty of the Sabbath is that it is God's gift to all of us—the poor and the oppressed as well as the rich and the privileged. When I was a child, like many poor families, my parents couldn't afford an annual vacation. They worked hard every day and my sister and I did well in school. Yet we never traveled to Disney World or the mountains, never visited an island or spent time in a cabin by a lake. Our vacation most years was a day trip to Atlantic City with a picnic lunch and, for my dad, a solo trip to visit his parents once a year in the South.

The Lord's sabbath honors families like mine with little privilege by saying you too are deserving of rest and renewal. A day to cease from your labors. Twenty-four hours to rest and play and sing. To enjoy it is an act of faith, a deliberate choice to believe that rather than wasting time, we are submitting to the necessity of investing it in ourselves and one another, to reflect on our history and the faithfulness of our God.

In the simplicity of sabbath, worship isn't an elaborate production. It is the acknowledgment in our hearts and minds of the God who has saved us, kept us, and guided us through another week. It is the creature calling out to the Creator with words of thanksgiving and acts of kindness. It is the weekly response to the daily invitation to come boldly before him with the living sacrifice of our bodies. It is searching to know what is that good, acceptable, and perfect plan determined for us. And it is the celebration of a life given to an undeserving and imperfect people with great love.

35

AND ONE FOR ALL

You [believers], like living stones,
are being built up into a spiritual house for a holy and
dedicated priesthood, to offer spiritual sacrifices [that are]
acceptable and pleasing to God through Jesus Christ.

1 PETER 2:5

TODAY I RAN INTO AN OLD FRIEND when I stopped to pick up lunch from a favorite spot. We chatted for a moment while I waited for my order and she shared how she was looking to return to church, a worshiping congregation, after being away from the Christian church for some time due to the ugliness that had become so prevalent. At the same time, she talked about how much she missed us— my husband and me—and how much our ministry had meant to her.

The conversation was a familiar one, and after I left her, I was again struck by the realization that my friend did not see me or my husband as "church." We were instead some rare other thing, disassociated from the Christian church as she knew it.

In frustration, I thought to myself, *I am church. We are church.* Why do we so readily accept the mean, evil, and ugly as church but disallow any expression of kindness or truth or grace in Jesus' name as the church, even as we shout that this is what the church ought to be?

According to biblical scholars, the word *church* is translated to mean "together," literally "in the same place at the same time," or *ecclesia*—a gathering, an assembly of believers. In light of this I have to concede that by myself I am not church, nor is any individual believer. It is only when we physically come together with other believers that we together become the church. "For where two or three are gathered in My name [meeting together as My followers], I am there among them" (Matthew 18:20). Of course, we know too that where two or three are gathered together, trouble is often in the midst as well. Gossip is in the midst. Hatred can be in the midst. Disagreements and lying, racism and abuse can be in the midst too. These are the potential hazards of human connection, yet an individual brick does not a house make.

Jesus declared that with himself as the bedrock or foundation, he would build the church, a called-out assembly of people who believe, like Peter, that Jesus is the Christ, the Messiah, the Son of the living God (Matthew 16:16). And these believers, later called by Peter "living stones," would come together to form a church so powerful that the gates of hell itself would not be able to withstand it.

A ton of bricks or stones—no matter how large or beautiful—strewn across the wilderness is useless, but stacked and held together with mortar, individual stones become structure, structure becomes building, building becomes shelter, and shelter can become a home that will last a hundred years or more.

Jesus said upon this rock, this God made flesh, this heaven come down, this demonstration of divine, unmerited, unconditional love, I will build my church. There are other churches out there, other assemblies of people who have set out to spew hatred and who bar their doors to the hungry and the stranger. Whitewashed tombs disguised as temples that house dead men's bones. These are not new or novel, but nor are they our only choice. As living stones, we may reassemble to form new worship communities and define the church as love and grace once again. We can read the old text through the new lens of those on the margins and reclaim a faith without flags or guns. And in the faces of friends and strangers we may just find ourselves.

I invited my friend to our place of worship that day and began praying that she would find her way to a place of love and belonging, one that more rightly reflected the God she knew. I prayed that she, with them, would become the church she was looking for so that others might find home in her as well.

Behold, I am laying in Zion a chosen stone, a precious (honored) Cornerstone, And he who believes in Him [whoever adheres to, trusts in, and relies on Him] will never be disappointed [in his expectations]. (1 Peter 2:6)

36

FROM FAITH TO FAITH

ONCE WATCHED A FILM depiction of Jesus healing the paralytic man who was let down through the roof by his friends. The story was framed to explain that one of those friends had been a witness to Jesus healing the leper, which resulted in a faith that Jesus could also heal her friend. The woman who witnessed the leper's healing was going about her everyday life and just happened to be in the path where Jesus was walking, just happened to overhear the man's pleas, just happened to see Jesus respond in love and power, and immediately faith was born.

At first I smirked at what I understood to be the writer's poetic license in connecting the two healing events, as they are not laid out so clearly in Scripture. But as I thought more about it the next day, I concluded that may very well have been how it happened. The friends did not randomly climb on top of a roof with a paralyzed man. Someone had heard or seen something of the power of God in the teaching and ministry of Jesus that had ignited their belief that Jesus was able to do the impossible and bring life to dead limbs.

We can spend a lot of time chasing after the bright and flashy, trying to catch a glimpse of something new or exciting. Or we can spend days ruminating with the deep, intellectual folks about how much more knowledgeable, inclusive, and evolved we are. Meanwhile, our families and neighborhoods remain in crisis. Our systems and societies go unchanged. However, if I instead keep showing up faithfully in the ordinary places of my everyday life, doing the mundane challenging things with anticipation, I may get to encounter the divine and witness the miraculous. Then faith grows in me and I am compelled to share the story and apply it to the needs in my own life and the lives of those around me.

Sometimes well-meaning teachers can imply that the journey of faith is a steady uphill climb toward a plateau of unwavering belief. I have rather found faith to be an ever-winding path over hills and towering mountains as well as down through dark and sometimes cavernous valleys. It is a road that provokes feelings of joyous victory as well as staggering defeat. However, if we persist through the sweat and the grief and the aching feet, we discover again and again that the journey is also what produces fruitfulness in our lives and results in our spiritual growth.

Evangelism is not about going door to door like holy salesmen with a pitch and a product. Witnessing is not about memorizing scripts or shouting at strangers through bullhorns. It is intentionally placing ourselves in the pathway of Jesus, on the everyday roads with the poor and the lame and the dying. It happens in the authentic conversations that emerge with a neighbor over meals or coffee. Or in the difficult work of creating new policies and the discomfort of changing harmful practices. It is testifying to what God has done from the sidelines of a soccer game, over FaceTime with a friend, or during a lunch break in the middle of a workday.

Recently, a friend posted an anniversary photo on Facebook of her and her spouse celebrating twenty-three years of love and marriage. When I saw it, I remembered the significant challenge they had faced in their relationship just a few years earlier and how God had healed and restored them. I have since shared God's faithfulness to them with someone else who was facing a similar situation. In relaying their story, I was sharing the gospel—the good news of God's miraculous healing—and that story served to birth and build faith in the life of someone else. Later I thought about the many Bible verses and inspiring quotes I've seen and read on social media and concluded that none of them preached a stronger message than that simple photo from my friend.

Marriage is hard, but every time God allows my husband and me to push past the petty and recommit to one another, we preach a sermon of God's faithfulness. Every day you testify to how God multiplied your bread, turned your water into wine, or healed your issue, you share the good news. Occasionally we may get to witness the miraculous—roofs ripped open, bodies lowered, and lifeless limbs healed. However, more often than not, it is marginalized people sharing meaningful stories of how God has shown up in their ordinary lives in extraordinary ways. This has always been God's most powerful medium. A servant at the wedding shares a story with a leper and the leper tells a brother how he was healed and the brother shares this hope with a struggling neighbor and the neighbor writes a letter to a friend. And it happens without a pulpit or a robe, outside the columns of the temple, between Sunday and the Sabbath, in the simple spaces of our lives.

39

HERO CAPES AND CAMOUFLAGE

While we were still helpless

[powerless to provide for our salvation],

at the right time Christ died [as a substitute]

for the ungodly.

ROMANS 5:6

WHY DO YOU NEED TO BE IN CONTROL? he asked. I did not answer. *Because you're afraid*, he went on. *What are you afraid of?*

"Failing," I whispered.

Not being loved. Not being accepted. Not being as good as you think or as people think you are, he said.

I remember when I was a child in elementary school, our classroom door would sometimes open and an aide would enter and approach the teacher's desk with a note from the office. If the paper was white, the message was generally informational and held no concern for us as students. But if the note was not white, all activity would cease and the room would go silent as the entire class held its collective breath. If the note was yellow, someone was being called down to the principal's office. If the note was pink, someone was being suspended! In either case, you did not want to hear your name called once the teacher got the colored note.

It was one of those mornings, one of those days when the activity in my devotional classroom had ceased because the note delivered from the Spirit had my name on it. Thankfully, pink slips are rare in God's schoolhouse. Our Lord is patient and suffers long with his children. But from time to time God calls us up to his office for a chat, and this was one of those days. When God is in the posture of correction, I feel every bit the size of my seven- or eight-year-old powerless self, and I bow my head and lower my eyes in reverence, but also in conviction, knowing I will again be seen and known, fully and completely in all my human frailty.

God has an office in the wilderness where degrees and titles offer no protection, where there are no fig leaves of busyness or flashy distractions of talent or personality to hide behind. In this barren landscape I can easily see what God has chosen to reveal—the truth of my fear. Through childhood experiences we learn how to be in the world, how to navigate, how to survive. As a child, I wasn't afraid of being seen. I was afraid of being rejected. So I learned two effective methods for avoiding that pain: invisibility and perfection. Be unseen or be the hero.

I learned to enter a room and quickly disappear into the safety and obscurity of the margins of the space, to listen intently, observe carefully, and to speak only when I had something substantial to say. In work it was dot every *i*, cross every *t*, and avoid making mistakes.

In the kingdom, neither of these mechanisms is useful or required. I am justified by faith. I have peace with God through Christ.

I have access to a grace that allows me to stand in hope. I have been reconciled—brought into agreement with the one who has given me this salvation. I do not need to hide or exhaust myself in the pursuit of perfection. The miseducation of the world teaches me I must earn love and acceptance. Racism and classism tell me I need to work twice as long and twice as hard to get half as much and, as a black woman who grew up poor, that what I get I don't deserve. Religion implies that I must keep the rules to gain God's love and avoid damnation. However, grace is not transactional. God proved his unconditional love by the fact that while we were still sinners, Christ died for us. And since we have now been declared free of the guilt of sin by his blood, we will be saved from the wrath of God through him.

I don't have to be the best and brightest student; the parent, spouse, or partner who is continually in control; or the leader afraid of being discovered as less than perfect. I have a God. I don't need to be one.

In God's office in the wilderness I am met with a love that dispels my fear, and I remember that I can have joy even in the arid conditions of this everyday life. Challenge produces patience and through patience I gain experience and through experience I have a hope that will not disappoint. Stripped of the hero cape and camouflage, I have room in the mercy and grace of God to risk and to fail and to try again. I am loved. I am accepted and forever reconciled to the God who made and chose me.

I am likely not as good as I am thought to be. But in him, I am enough.

38

FINDING FAITH IN
A FOREIGN LAND

O N A RECENT SUMMER SABBATICAL, my husband chose to spend his time off writing in a foreign country. Since technology allows us to work from almost anywhere, I tagged along—have laptop, will travel. We booked a long-term Airbnb and bought one-way plane tickets since we planned to return from a different country at the end of our trip.

It was both scary and exciting to step off a plane in an unfamiliar place knowing we would not be returning home anytime soon. We gathered our luggage, exchanged our US dollars for the local currency, and headed outside to look for transportation. All around us was the hum of words we did not understand, signs we could not read in a language unknown to us. Still, before long we climbed into the back of a rideshare, exhausted from the long flight but wide-awake with anticipation.

We have come to love international travel. It is the opportunity to say goodbye to life as we know it and immerse ourselves in a people and culture different from our own. We generally avoid hotels or fancy resorts filled with American tourists. Instead, we opt for rental properties tucked in the middle of community. There we have the opportunity to shop in the markets, walk to local cafés, and talk to native people who are working, playing, and living their everyday lives. It forces us out of the comfort of the familiar in a way that takes us off autopilot, making us pause and reflect on what we eat, wear, and listen to—and why. We are reintroduced to art and music, made to look at history through a different lens, and invited to consider the origin of our own customs, values, and behaviors. If we stay long enough, we begin to reimagine our futures and our way of living.

It takes a couple of days to break our minds free from the clock and the calendar, but soon we are able to respond to questions about time and date with, "Who cares?" and "It doesn't matter." We are careful not to cram our days with preplanned activity but rather to leave time for unforeseen adventures and unexpected joy. We wander, get lost, and then are found again.

> So Moses said, "I must turn away [from the flock] and see this great sight." . . . When the LORD saw that he turned away [from the flock] to look, God called to him from the midst of the bush. (Exodus 3:3-4)

In one such wandering, I discovered God. Again. Atop a hill in Paris, among the stone arched ceilings, stained glass, and whispered prayers of the Sacre-Coeur Basilica. It was over thirty-seven hundred miles and an ocean away from the church I knew. Here, the sermon was in Latin and the parishioners spoke French—and Portuguese and English and Italian, German and Arabic, Swahili and Zulu. The confessions of sinners moved from stories to real life, ordered by a

posted schedule outside a small, carved wooden booth. Here God
was bigger than the pulpit space marked off by my former church's
velvet ropes. God was higher than the lofty arguments of the well-
known Western seminaries. Here, for me, God was not bound by a
single idea, understanding, or practice. He had escaped the borders
of print and page. In this place without the limits of time and date or
the chains of our finite understanding, God was free to be God. God
moved outside my boxes and spread unapologetically into the unlimited, open space of I Am.

Everything we know of God has been shaped by a concept and
context too small. Everything associated with him—love, truth,
justice, and grace—has been bent and contorted to squeeze inside
the parameters of a sinful human imagination that limits such
things to the powerful few. Our understanding of community, family,
and church may be distorted or incomplete. Sometimes, often, God's
plumb line stretches beyond the walls of our tiny self-made existence. To do the work of justice we may need to raise the ceiling or
open up some walls to bring ourselves and all of creation into
alignment with the divine design and purposes of God.

In the wilderness, we can choose to move deliberately beyond the
tourist areas of our Christian circles into the real-life, sometimes
challenging communities that surround them. We can remove the
barricades from our churches, correct the teachings of our pharisees,
and push ourselves past the boundaries of our comfort zones.

This is not an excuse to cast off everything we have known of God
before. But rather to leave our hands, hearts, and minds open to discover him beyond the fences and borders of our previous knowledge.
It is an invitation to question what we think we know and open

ourselves to the possibility of a more excellent way. To stand firmly on the sure foundations of our most holy faith while looking ever upward toward a more perfect knowledge of Christ, our neighbors, and ourselves. This is an invitation to return to the Way with fresh eyes. To wander, get lost, and be found again.

39

LET THERE BE RAIN

"For my thoughts are not your thoughts,

Nor are your ways My ways," declares the LORD.

ISAIAH 55:8

GREW UP IN A FOUR-SEASON northeastern city and then spent sixteen years in the southern Atlanta sun before moving to the Pacific Northwest. Before that, rain was an occasional irritation. Something that showed up to ruin recess, baseball games, hairstyles, and family picnics. It was never met with anything that resembled joy or appreciation. But living in Oregon for eleven years expanded my view of the rain.

I watched my neighbors welcome the rain that showed up each fall like it was a well-loved friend. They seemed to greet it as an annual invitation to slow down and get reacquainted with books and movies and game nights with close friends. They bragged about the beauty of their green plants and trees through the months of winter when elsewhere everything was brown. And they laughed and shook their heads at what they saw to be the unnecessary struggles of those of us insistent on using umbrellas.

In the wilderness—this waiting room between the faith and life we knew and the one that is not yet—we have the opportunity to look again at things we previously evaluated and dismissed. To pick up last month's magazine and flip through its pages. We stare again at the well-known pictures on the wall and handle the fabric of the familiar chairs. And sometimes in the agony of those slow, drawn-out waiting room minutes, we discover something we had not seen before. We remember a detail previously read but not absorbed, previously seen and yet overlooked. We reencounter a word or image or thread in the pattern that captures our attention and allows us to be moved or challenged or impacted again. Like young children again discovering the rain.

Silently now, we may begin to question ourselves. When did I become so cynical, so angry, so self-righteous? Where did I lose the wonder and curiosity of this life? How did I become the person who gazes out the windows of my life and sees only problems rather than the miracle and divine blessing of the rain?

One afternoon I sat at my desk on the second floor of the old Portland church where my office was located, annoyed by the noise rising outside my window. It was midafternoon and raining, as it did most afternoons this time of year. But the yard of the elementary school across the street had just filled with children who had come outside for recess. I stared out the window in annoyed amazement. The children were running and laughing and screaming in play. They climbed and jumped and chattered incessantly.

What's wrong with them? I thought. *Don't they know it's raining?*

When I was kid and it rained at my West Philadelphia elementary school, outdoor recess was usually canceled and we played inside in the gym or remained in our classrooms. But these kids were playing and laughing as though there was no rain. I shook my head in confusion and tried to return to my writing but my eyes kept shifting to the schoolyard.

Before too long a thought occurred to me. If they waited for it to stop raining here, they would almost never go outside. This is how my grown-up Portland neighbors and friends became who they are—lovers of gray skies and downpours. They were children who learned to play in the rain. Their parents dressed them in rubber boots and waterproof hooded jackets with thin warm layers underneath. Their weather forecasters didn't describe the skies as "threatening," and social and sporting events were seldom "rained out." The rain was not an annoyance or something to be avoided but a natural part of their lives, like fog and wind and sunshine. More than that, it was the gift that gave them the many parks and lakes and waterfalls they loved to visit and a necessity for the fresh produce and delicious food for which the city is known.

The concrete yard behind my childhood home did not require water. In the urban landscape where I grew up, parks, lakes, and waterfalls were few to none. I realized that day how context had shaped my opinion and behavior and caused me to resent and abandon that which God had meant for good. How many of us have abandoned people, places, or things we may have found significant or fulfilling? How much have we discarded as negative or useless what could have been enjoyed? What beauty have we walked away from? What gifts, once loved, do we now frown upon with disdain? We gaze out through our blurry windows with annoyance and grumble with scoffing irritation at those who've returned to them.

Perhaps, in the wandering and waiting periods of our lives, God is drawing our attention. Inviting us to consider again some of the things we've dismissed as worthless or unnecessary. Bidding us to flip through the pages and retrace the lines and handle again the fabric of our faith. To open our mouths and lift our scrunched-up faces to the sky and taste again and see that, even in the places we've abandoned, God is still good.

Even after a decade, I cannot say I ever came to enjoy the rain of my Northwest home. But I did realize that my concept of rain had been shaped by my prior context and expectations, and that I'd had to move to another space and live there long enough to see the rain in a new way.

> For as the rain and snow come down from heaven,
> And do not return there without watering the earth,
> Making it bear and sprout,
> And providing seed to the sower and bread to the eater,
>
> So will My word be which goes out of My mouth;
> It will not return to Me void (useless, without result),
> Without accomplishing what I desire,
> And without succeeding in the matter for which I sent it.
> (Isaiah 55:10-11)

40

MIRRORS

WHEN I MOVED BACK TO ATLANTA after eleven years in the predominantly white Pacific Northwest, my self-concept improved almost immediately. Seeing myself reflected in the voluptuous curves and bronze tones of the "black mecca" brought an almost instant boost to my self-esteem. I sat up a little taller hearing the resonant voices from my car radio and the familiar bump and sway of R&B. I found myself smiling as I stepped back into the black girl magic and attitude I once knew.

But then I paused, reflecting on the difference I felt, the smile melting into a frown. An uncomfortable question came from the Spirit to my mind. Was I finding my worth in the images around me? Getting my value from human reflections in the world?

There has been much discussion around the need to "see ourselves" reflected in the various roles of our society. This idea definitely has merit and is invaluable to enlarging our imaginations around our place in the world. But while these images are useful for adding options for our consideration, they should not be relied upon to determine our value or worth.

The world's mirror is not real. It is image and reflection of light. We look for it to tell us who we should be or who we are becoming. We look for our reflection in the eyes of others, expecting them to tell us who we are. But the world's mirrors show us only outward appearance, reflecting back our flat, two-dimensional shapes, patterns, and colors as we present them to the world.

Looking at my mirror reflections, I can temporarily adjust what I see. I brush or slick down the stray hairs, suck in the protruding belly, and cover the blemishes under color-matched concealers. I can stretch my neck or lengthen my legs with the right shirt or hemline. Hide the grays or thinning hair with permanent color or the perfect hat. But the inward flaws are harder to conceal. Laziness and insecurity, impatience, greed, and arrogance. We can hide it all behind pleasant smiles and gentle tones for just so long before our dark natural roots begin to show.

We sometimes hide this darkness with bright, shiny outward things, pursuing riches and possessions to gain temporary admiration, a weak insufficient substitute for unconditional love. We buy logos and create brands, produce reels and TikTok dances. Finding significance in the applause of followers—most of them strangers we will never know. But image cannot carry us through the harsh challenges of this life. It is candy glass, easily shattered and swept away.

Achievement is another imposter promising fulfillment and satisfaction. Name on a plaque, statue on a shelf, calling us the first, the best, or the greatest of all time. We don the T-shirt or wear the medal. Lift the golden calf above our head. But the moment quickly passes. The image blurs and then we're off again chasing the next achievement to help us tell the distorted, fragmented story of who we are.

By contrast, the Word of God is less a mirror and more a laparoscope, shining its light into our innermost parts. It reveals the true contents of our minds and hearts and holds them up against the perfect standard of God's design found in the person of Jesus. Staring into my own heart through the scope of God's Word, Spirit diagnoses disease and begins the process of transformation. It shifts my gaze from endless comparison with others to imitation of the one true Christ.

> He made from one man every nation of mankind to live on the face of the earth, having determined their appointed times and the boundaries of their lands and territories. This was so that they would seek God, if perhaps they might grasp for Him and find Him, though He is not far from each one of us. For in Him we live and move and exist [that is, in Him we actually have our being], as even some of your own poets have said, "For we also are His children." (Acts 17:26-28)

When I identify him as the Christ, then I can bow in humble submission. When I identify him as the Christ, then I abandon all other idols and gods. When I identify with him as the Christ, I strive daily to change not so much my outward appearance, but my thoughts, attitudes, and behavior to align with his teaching and to resemble his love. When I identify with him as the Christ, I prioritize his mission and message above my own.

And in time these actions and practices begin to re-form me, to transform me into a being after his likeness. And I discover my true value, myself, in the immutable one, fearfully and wonderfully made. Beautiful in every city.

Epilogue

CROSSING JORDAN

ON COUNTLESS AIRLINE FLIGHTS I've marked the ten thousand feet milestone by pulling out a phone or laptop and settling back in my chair, rarely taking notice of the beauty outside the coveted window seat. But on a recent visit to the island of Maui, we made our way to those heights outside the walls of a plane. The highest point on the island is the summit of a volcano, Haleakala. It towers at 10,023 feet and can be reached by car up a long, winding road and then a short walk. On my sixty-first birthday we decided to drive up for the rare opportunity to stand on the earth above the clouds.

Twice on the way up we drove through dense fog and light rain, and each time I thought we should turn back. I was afraid we would make the effort and the two-hour-plus drive only to be disappointed, our view blocked by thick gray clouds as we stood shivering in the rain. But as this was our last day in Hawaii and this ride our only plan for the day, we made the decision to drive on.

At just over nine thousand feet we reached the visitors center. Here again we considered making ourselves content with this milestone and heading back down. But the few colorful pictures and tourist trinkets didn't seem worth the drive. When we came out of the center, the sky looked a little brighter and the rain slowed and then stopped, so we climbed back in the car and continued on. Soon, at the gated entrance to the national park, we were asked to pay a fee. Thirty dollars for a three-day pass, knowing we would be on a flight out the next morning. We grudgingly paid the price and pushed on, up the road, around the curves, on lanes that felt precariously close to the edge of a steep and dangerous drop. We continued until the gray clouds fell beneath us and a warm sun and blue skies appeared above. Immediately at that sight, a prayer fell from my lips. "It was worth it."

In the Exodus story, the wilderness was a special, hard place. It was where the Israelites re-established their identity, as the people of God rather than Egyptian slaves. It was where they witnessed God's grace, punishment, and power. It was where their doubts, fears, and idolatry were exposed and where those who refused to repent died away. Finally, it was where a new generation, leaning into their identity as God's people, crossed over into the Promised Land.

In this present day, it appears that the people of God are once again in a wilderness place, trekking breathlessly between the shame of the past and the hopeful promise of a distant future. Perhaps this present time, with its many challenges, is also an opportunity to reestablish our identity in him. To rediscover the riches of unconditional love and the gift of unmerited favor. Perhaps these years in the desert are reminding us of the God we once knew and the church we are called to be. To give us the opportunity to reconnect with our main love as our first love and ourselves as his chosen bride.

Certainly the climb is steep and the road seems long, and many times we consider turning back. And even now the skies of our faith may be clouded and filled with certain rain. Besides all that, the cost seems too high and the promised return on investment unsure. But I encourage you to hang in there with God and his people even if all you have left is the whisper of his word and the faint breath of his Spirit. In a few more turns we're going to clear these clouds and this annoying rain and incessant darkness will begin to fall away.

As I discovered that day on my climb to the summit of Haleakala, when you are again standing in the warmth and beauty of his holiness, you will thank God not for that moment but for the climb. It was worth it to be reminded that there is still more to see in this life. There is still more to do. And while there will certainly be wind and rain and times when life's fog is so thick you can barely see ten feet in front of you, pay the price. Keep going. Because when you least expect it, the rain will stop. The clouds will thin and the light you almost forgot will suddenly reappear. Best of all, the God who loves you will be there waiting in the face of a Promised Land sun.

NOTES

12. Imposter Syndrome

[1]Kajal Matkhare, "'I am not good enough.' How many of you have had this feeling in your professional life?" LinkedIn post, August 12, 2023, www.linkedin.com/posts/kajal-matkhare-479364188_imposter syndrome-impostersyndrome-sundaymusings-activity-70963124277 88533760-uc6j.

15. Hungry in the Far Country

[1]Vineyard Worship featuring Kathryn Scott, "Hungry (Falling on My Knees)," YouTube, July 17, 2014, www.youtube.com/watch?v=erQku5 -OOY0.

33. A Familiar Feast

[1]Martin Luther King, speech at the Washington National Cathedral, March 31, 1968, www.nps.gov/mlkm/learn/quotations.htm.

ALSO BY THE AUTHOR

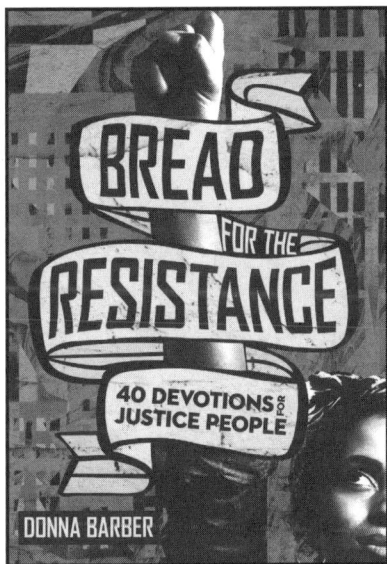

Bread for the Resistance
978-0-8308-4396-1

THE VOICES PROJECT

The Voices Project gathers leaders of color who influence culture (the church, education, art, entertainment, politics, and business) for important conversations about the current challenges and triumphs within communities of color and our role as cultural influencers. We train and promote leaders of color to offer voice to culture and society.

TRAINING AND PROMOTING

We provide insight on how to be effective in leadership within one's respective area of cultural influence in a way that is rooted in the history and experience of people of color. Additionally we connect leaders of color to leadership opportunities that are based in their areas of expertise within a domain of cultural influence.

INITIATIVES

- Mentoring
- Publishing
- Leadership gatherings (trainings, workshops, conferences, retreats, pilgrimage)
- Internships

THE VOICES PROJECT
PO Box 6512
Atlanta, GA 30315
www.voices-project.org/

 https://x.com/jointhevoices

 www.facebook.com/JoinTheVoices/

 www.instagram.com/jointhevoices/